WHO DO YOU SAY I AM?
The Christ story in the cosmic context

"The first and last task of every leader is to keep hope alive"(John Gardner). Kevin Treston is such a leader, and his latest book, Who do you say that I am? *is the bearer of hope.*

Kevin keeps hope alive by offering his readers a new paradigm for understanding the Christian story. He is respectful of past paradigms but has realised that they are too limited to take us forward. The new is elsewhere. Christianity has reached a point of no return.

In what resides our hope? Kevin Treston lays out his reasoning that our emerging consciousness about our ever expanding cosmos holds the key. This consciousness opens us to a new understanding of the Christ event, and its implications for cosmic creation, especially humanity, and for Christianity in particular.

If you feel the need to enliven your faith, enlarge your hope, and enrich your love, then read this book. You won't be disappointed!

Garry Everett

Kevin Treston's most recent book Who Do You Say I Am?: The Christ Story in the Cosmic Context *is a timely contribution to theological conversations concerning ultimate questions about creation and being. Kevin argues that the Augustinian fall/ restoration theology, premised on the Genesis myth, no longer connects with the lived experience of 21st century truth 'seekers'. The challenge of reconciling the science/religion relationship demands a 'starting point' for the Christian story that incorporates the evolutionary story of the universe. Notions of a Cosmic Christ merge theology of the early church fathers with that of contemporary theologians such as Teilhard de Chardin. In both instances humans 'made in the image and likeness of God' and through a process of 'Christogenesis' evolve with the potential to grow in God's likeness.*

Kevin Treston's ability to communicate complex theology in simplified accessible language is a boon to Study of Religion and religious educators generally. RE teachers often struggle to connect disinterested westerners with the profound truths of the Christian tradition. Kevin's 'Cosmic Christian Story' complements the works of renowned religious education authors such as Peter Vardy and Albert Nolan's interpretation of Jesus. Kevin Treston asks, 'In the light of modern cosmology and science, can the incarnation be comprehended outside the great story of the universe?'

Steve Jorgensen

WHO DO YOU SAY I AM?

The Christ story in the cosmic context

KEVIN TRESTON

MORNING STAR PUBLISHING

Published in Australia by
Morning Star Publishing
P. O. Box 51
Northcote Vic. 3070
Australia

ISBN 9780995381520

Copyright © Kevin Treston 2016

All rights reserved. Other than for the purposes and subject to the conditions prescribed under the *Copyright Act*, no part of this publication may be reproduced, stored in a retrieval system, or transmitted in any form or by any means, electronic, mechanical, photocopying, recording or otherwise, without the prior permission of the publisher.

Unless otherwise noted, Scripture quotations are taken from the *New Revised Standard Version Bible*, copyright 1989, Division of Christian education of the national Council of Churches of Christ in the United States of America. Used by permission. All rights reserved.

First published 2016

Cataloguing-in-Publication entry is available from the National Library of Australia http:/catalogue.nla.gov.au/.

Typesetting by John Healy
Printed in Australia

Contents

Introduction 7

Chapter One 11
A selection of dilemmas for Western Christianity

Chapter Two 39
Context issues in the Traditional Christian Story

Chapter Three 47
The Fall/Redemption Traditional Christian Story

Chapter Four 65
Features of a Cosmic Christian Story: the beginnings

Chapter Five 77
Understanding the Cosmic Christian Story

Chapter Six 87
Daily living the Cosmic Christian Story

Chapter Seven 119
Gatherings

Reflections 125

Introduction

This book, *Who Do You Say I Am?* (Mark 8:29) is intended for Christians who are seeking to make their Christian beliefs more intelligible in the modern world of evolutionary science and cosmology. The core theme of the book is an exploration of the Christ story within a cosmological vision as a complementary story to the Traditional Christian Story. Such an enterprise is not simply an esoteric intellectual theological exercise but a proposal towards deepening a faith commitment to a Christ experience, leading to engagement with the wider world.

The inspiration for this book has arisen out of my sixty years of ministry in several countries and listening to the stories of people in their quest for a vital Christian faith. Increasingly, I have encountered a widespread disillusionment with the institutional church in Western countries which seems incapable of or unwilling to make significant changes in its structures in the face of dominant intrusive consumerism and cultural relativism. Christianity, at least in the West, seems generally to have lost much of its vitality and relevance to life. There appears to be a widespread feeling that the church is out of step with the realities of ordinary life. It is imperative that Christianity reformulate its beliefs and liturgical practices which resonate with the world of evolutionary science, globalisation, internet, cosmology, spirituality and the social sciences. Above all, to respond to the *cri de coeur* of people who are searching for spiritual sustenance and ways to deepen their relationships with a loving God.

There is an emerging consciousness which invites a Christian narrative to develop an alternative orthodoxy to the current orthodoxy of church teachings. Above all, the Christian community must be a community of meaningful relationships. A realignment of beliefs and practices is not some internal religious tinkering with doctrines but a Spirit endeavour to energise the practice of Christian faith according to an alternative orthodoxy which I name as the Cosmic Christian Story.

In recent years, I have been increasingly fascinated by the wondrous vision of the universe illuminated through modern studies of cosmology and astrophysics. Religions are challenged to reframe their beliefs within this cosmic appreciation of the universe. If God as Source of Being has created and energises this vast universe, who are we within the web of life in this universe and what is our destiny? How does the Christ story as currently being told resonate with the overarching story of the universe? How have science and technology changed the very way we think? Modern science, especially quantum physics, offers possible pathways for Christians to reframe their great Story of God's revelation in Jesus. For Christians, how does the new consciousness shape the Christian narrative? Is enhancing planetary health now emerging as a critical moral imperative for all religions and all people?

Scholars describe how the Jewish, Roman and Greek context of the traditional Jesus story fashioned the genre of how the story of Jesus as the Christ was told and communicated.

For Christians, a key question is, 'What (was) is the mission of Jesus?'

While preserving the essentials of the Christian faith, can the Jesus narrative be told and lived within another religious frame of reference? Is there an alternative, endorsed orthodoxy which complements the orthodoxy of the Fall/Redemption narrative? This book proposes a 'yes' to that question.

A possible framework for Christian beliefs and faith life begins, not with the purported failure of God's original plan through the sin of Adam and Eve, but with God's revelation in the creation of the universe. Christ is to be understood within the evolutionary process of the whole universe. While God's revelation in Jesus is explored as a Cosmic Christian Story, it is also important to affirm the Traditional Christian Story as the primal story for God's revelation in Jesus.

This book is intended for those who aspire to deepen their Christian faith within a world of the interrelationship of all things. In my conferences over the years, I have found an almost unbridgeable chasm between what is discussed in theological circles and what beliefs people on the ground espouse. There is also a fading interest in matters religious at least in its institutional form in the West. A diminishing number of people in the West who profess a Christian faith are struggling to find viable expressions of their Christian faith. An increasingly educated Christian population will not be convinced by exhortations about the necessity of obedience to the teachings of the church which never change. The church no longer controls information about its beliefs. The internet has bypassed historical theological monopolies thus enabling people now to verify or dispute official church proclamations. Authority is credible only if that authority is transparent and truthful.

In this book, I have sought to avoid becoming entangled in theological controversy. My desire is to offer pathways of being Christian today. This book is for general readers and hence I have tried to simplify complex religious issues. The book is also a useful resource for tertiary students, teachers of religious education and Studies of Religion (SOR).

The growing number of people who profess no religious belief at all challenges any fanciful view of Western countries as being culturally religious. Research shows a marked increase in atheism and indifference to church related matters. Christian fundamentalism has no real interest in 'Cosmic Christians Stories'. The growing pluralism of religious faiths reinforces the wide diversity of religious faiths in multicultural societies. While commitment to the institutional aspects of church is diminishing in the West, there seems to be an emerging interest and participation in spirituality. The question must be asked, 'How does the Christ story engage people with this aspiration towards spirituality?'

Although the cultural context of the book is being Christian in a Western orientated country, my pastoral experiences in developing countries would suggest that some of the themes discussed have definitive relevance in those countries. For Christians in non-Western countries such as Africa and Asia, there may be other pressings concerns for living their Christian lives.

The topic of the book is not new. For example, Matthew Fox's book *Original Blessing*, published in 1983, explored one aspect of this topic, the Fall/Redemption model of Christianity. Adrian Smith's *A New Framework for Christian Belief* (2001) is relevant to themes in this book. There are a plethora of resources on this topic. This book is a successor to my previous book *Emergence for Life Not Fall from Grace: Making Sense of the Jesus Story in the Light of Evolution*. Since the publication of the book (2013) the themes in the book have been extended within the current cultural climate and rapid scientific advances. What concerns me is how scant is the familiarity with the themes in the book in the lives of ordinary Christians. Prophetic voices calling for significant church renewal struggle to make their voices heard within a culture of doctrinal conformity. All too often the response of a younger generation is either a return to a parallel fundamentalism, a rejection of Christian beliefs as some kind of irrelevant relic of past times or studied indifference to the whole topic of religion itself. Another response is a quest for a free-floating genre of spirituality without a firm doctrinal base.

The focus question that acts as a stimulus for this book is:

What is the starting point for the Christian narrative?

Is the impulse for the Incarnation:

An act of restoration by Jesus for a failure in God's original plan of creation?

or

Jesus as the Christ within the dynamic evolution of God's creation?

In the composition of this book, I owe much to all those who have shared their wisdoms over the years and challenged the limits of my own thinking.

In particular I wish to thank Steve Jorgensen, Helen Treston, Ross Keane, Gary Curran, Ron Holmes, Garry Everett, Patrick Oliver, John Coles, Laraine Roberts, Yuri Koszarycz, Adrian Bellamore.

I wish to acknowledge my indebtedness to a whole host of authors especially Ilia Delio, Thomas Berry, Matthew Fox, Denis Edwards, Diarmuid O'Murchu, Elizabeth Johnson, Judy Cannato, Charles Taylor, Ken Wilber, Adam Smith and Richard Rohr. Each of the authors listed in 'Resources' has been helpful in my own research.

George Kendall has been a steady source of assistance in the general composition of the book.

The team at Morning Star Publishing – Nick Mattiske, Hugh McGinlay and John Healy - have been professional and helpful in preparing the book for publication.

However, opinions in the book are mine and do not reflect the views of the people named.

Reflection questions are included for personal faith development and small group discussion groups. I would encourage readers to gather small groups to reflect and discuss the questions in each section of the book.

A special thanks to Kathryn for her unfailing support in all my writings.

Kevin Treston 2016

Chapter One

A selection of dilemmas for Western Christianity

We acknowledge and live our lives in and through stories, the bones upon which we hang the flesh of our lives. We have acknowledged, as Thomas Berry has pointed out, that our generation is one that is between stories - between the scientific and religious, between the old and the new. But the other side - the place where all stories can meet and dialogue and discover their common truths - is in sight.

Judy Cannato,
Fields of Compassion: How the New Cosmology is Transforming Spiritual Life, 145.

Surely one of the most provocative questions in the whole of the New Testament is asked by Jesus, *'Who do you say I am?'* (Mark 8:29).

What is your response to this question?

This question has been answered by billions of Christians throughout the ages. Their responses vary from ethnic group to ethnic group, from people in one era to another, from unbelievers to devout followers of Christ. Western civilisation has been significantly shaped by the answer to that question.

For contemporary Christians, a core question is, 'What is God saying to us through God's revelation to humankind and creation through Jesus as the Christ?'

It is an expectation that this book offers further responses to this question in the light of an evolutionary perspective on creation.

One may also turn the question, *Who do you say I am?* around to direct the question to oneself, 'Who am I in this world now?', 'What is happening in our cultural environment?', 'What are the crunch concerns in justice and planetary health?', 'Where do I encounter God or do I encounter God at all?', 'How significant for my spirituality is being a member of the church?', 'How do I not just know about God, but *experience* God?'

There is also a more radical challenge of wondering if the whole question of beliefs is really a crucial issue in the face of global poverty, environmental degradation, a flood of refugees, terrorism and a loss of a cultural spiritual narrative. A person struggling with basic questions of life might well ask,

'Why bother at all about what I believe in if I can't pay for food for my children or if I am homeless?'

For those who work among a younger generation of Christians there is also a question of the apparent irrelevance of beliefs about the Christian faith. What is happening in their lives now may seem far removed from the Christ story. Do the philosophical and scientific assumptions underpinning the Traditional Christian Story still make sense to people of the upcoming generation? These people are maturing in a developing world shaped by science, global technology and evolutionary consciousness.

I would strongly affirm that everyone needs a profound story to live by. For Christians, there is a need for the Jesus story to makes sense in a rapidly changing and anxious world. To live without a meaningful story that touches the heart is to wearily climb a stairway of nihilism and despair. The cultural anxiety in Western society is now intertwined with the collapse of a global meta-narrative (universal story). The meta-narrative of Western civilisation for over a thousand years was the Christian story. Such a previous overarching narrative had deep spiritual foundations that offered coherent responses to the great questions of life, especially to the axial question, 'What does it mean to live if one day I will die?' Today, there is a pluralism of conflicting cultural stories, many of these stories forged out of ideologies of consumerism and devoid of spiritual depths, barren wastelands of failed dreams.

Christians believe that the Incarnation (Latin: *carne* 'flesh') is a fusion of the human and the divine in the person of Jesus as the Christ. A response to the question of Jesus, *Who do you say I am?* encourages a rejoinder from Christians that is both an expression of faith in God's revelation in Jesus and an awareness of one's own being in life situations. In his book *New Seeds of Contemplation*, a Trappist monk Thomas Merton (d 1968) wrote, 'To be a saint means to be myself. Therefore, the problem of sanctity and salvation is, in fact, the finding out who I am and discovering my true self' (31).

There are three elements for Christians in any discourse about the significance of the Christ story:

- God
- Self
- Cosmos

A major challenge for Christianity in the 21st century is to restore the right relations between these three elements. The notion of 'self' is inflated or distorted in the West. God is dispatched into the realm of irrelevance and a major crisis in cosmos has left planet earth reeling from ecological vandalism. All too often in the Christian story God has been imaged as a Towering Judge, self has been birth-marked by original sin and the cosmos hung as a mere backdrop on the stage of human drama. A pressing enterprise for Christians today is bringing together God, self and cosmos into a providential vision of harmony.

How these three elements are in relationships with one another is explored in the following chapters. The discourse about these elements proposes a contemporary cosmic framework of beliefs about Jesus who is the Christ.

I begin the exploration of the topic by discussing a series of dilemmas that impact on the composition of a framework of beliefs and religious practices. The discussion of certain contemporary dilemmas is followed by an outline and critique of the traditional way of telling the Christ story. I name this narrative the 'Traditional Christian Story'. This story represents a position of current orthodoxy for those in the Christian church.

I will then outline and discuss an alternative orthodoxy which I name the 'Cosmic Christian Story'.

The selection of a series of dilemmas reflects current issues about Christianity. Each dilemma is a critical concern for those who are interested in promoting the Christ story and experience. Each dilemma offers opportunities for the Good News if the dilemmas are acknowledged and creatively addressed by open Christian communities.

How the question, *Who do you say I am?* is answered will shape the future of Christianity in Western culture and possibly offer a global vision of God's revelation in Jesus for harmony in world civilisation.

Four pivotal questions guide the genre of this book:

- How might the Christ story be best told and lived within the unfolding story of creation?
- What does it mean for me today to be a Christian in a world of religious pluralism and diverse patterns of cultural beliefs?
- What beliefs shape the ways I hope to live a Christian life?
- How do I live a wholesome life for myself, others and planetary wellbeing?

Let us consider some dilemmas that are pertinent to the topic of the Christ Story.

The dilemma of an open or closed response to cultural challenges

Studies on religion in Western countries show a steady decline in church affiliation, liturgical practice and commitment to institutional religion generally. There is research in Britain to indicate that England can no longer be regarded as a Christian country (see Report of Butler-Sloss Commission 2015). The 2013 census data in UK showed that 42% of the population were Christians and 22% of Christians were 65 years or older. The professor of sociology of religion at Lancaster University, Linda Woodhead, highlighted how research showing that those professing 'no religion' ('Nones') is becoming more the norm for young people (British Academy Lecture 19/2/2016). The 2013 census data in UK found that 49% professed 'no religion'. In countries such as Australia, New Zealand and Canada, similar patterns of disengagement from religion are prevalent. The social researcher and writer Krista Tippett in USA writes about the growing number of 'Nones' who have a strong spiritual orientation that is firmly grounded in their quest for a holistic way of living their humanity without any specific commitment to an institutional form of religion. She estimates that 23% of people in USA are Nones. Even in a traditional Catholic country such as Italy, only 50% of people now profess to be Catholic. There is now great diversity in the narratives and symbols by which people interpret their living realities. The age of shared Christian cultural norms and unifying symbols in the West has largely dissipated.

The so-called 'detraditionalisation' of Christianity in Europe is well documented in studies that show a significant movement away from institutional Christianity (Boeve: 2005). The concept of detraditionalisation refers to how the traditions of a religion are no longer being passed on to the next generation. Religious disaffiliation is now becoming a common issue within families. More and more people are becoming, in the words of Grace Davie, 'believing without belonging' (quoted in Boeve 2005:102). It would seem that God has gone into exile from many churches but paradoxically has taken up residence in other more friendly places. The whereabouts of these 'more friendly places' will be discussed later.

The reasons for the decline in church affiliation are exceedingly complex and relate to social, ethnic and cultural factors as well as the state of

Christianity itself. The movement from shared communal cultural values to an individualistic secular culture militates against church identity and active membership. European studies show only one third of those interviewed believe in a personal God rather than some Spirit or Force (Boeve 2005: 110). The prevailing 'pick-and-choose' cultural norms among a younger generation generate a fluid approach to any long term religious commitment, to say nothing about a growing unapologetic atheism. The ghosts of the dictum *sapere aude* ('work it out yourself') of the philosopher Immanuel Kant (1724 -1804) still haunt the corridors of modernity. The principle of *sapere aude* eschews any authority telling a person what to do or believe. Social ethical issues such as same-sex marriages, euthanasia, abortion, IVF and genetic modification are debated in the public arena with scant reference to the teachings of the churches. The era of a tribal and socially isolated Christianity is over. The twin foundations of Roman law and Greek philosophy which traditionally described Christian life have largely been exiled by post-modern thinking. In our time, Christianity will either proactively participate in the ebbs and flows of the lives of people or will gradually be relegated to a tribal relic of past times, at least in Western countries.

The rigidity of the churches to transform their structures and their failure to modify teachings that seem to be at variance with the spirit of Jesus, reinforce feelings of alienation from the institutional aspects of Christianity. Such rigidity in a rapidly changing social environment tends to isolate the churches from being a significant voice in discourse within the moral pluralism of local communities. Christian groups that hold a firm line on issues such as subordinate status of women, discrimination against gay and lesbian people, divorce and remarriage, culture of clericalism, dysfunctional church structures, infallibility of teachings (*magisterium ordinarium*) and exclusion of prophetic voices, all such issues risk diminishing the effectiveness of proclaiming the gospel. The intransigence of the church to initiate discerned renewal accelerates the decline in church membership in Western orientated countries.

A contrary viewpoint on the stance of the churches to public ethical dilemmas is expressed in a steadfast refusal by some church leaders to compromise a fidelity to the perceived venerable teachings of the church. For those who insist on upholding traditional beliefs and ethical teachings, the movement to succumb to the temptation of becoming 'relevant' is nothing less than a betrayal of perceived timeless Christian teachings. Conservative thinking believes it is more authentic to uphold a 'pure church' rather than support one which has prostituted itself to accommodate the latest social, politically correct ideology. It is also interesting to note as a counter to the decline of commitment to institutional religion in the West, projections estimate that China will be the largest Christian country by the middle of this century and the number of people across the globe professing affiliation to some form of religion is actually increasing not declining.

There is surely no need to emphasise the dedication of so many Christians and their commitment to the common good. The wellbeing of people and culture generally would be seriously diminished without the services offered by the churches and individual Christians. The heroic commitment of pastors and lay people to justice and peace is attested by everyday service and caring agencies. Western culture is immensely indebted to its Judaeo-Christian heritage. When we reflect on the abundance of cultural richness inspired by a Christian ethos, we give thanks for this incredible heritage. Just imagine our cultural heritage without such people and religious expressions as Simone Weil, the paintings of Caravaggio and da Vinci, the 'Requiem' of Mozart, Hildegard of Bingen, monasteries, Francis of Assisi, Hayden's 'Alleluia' chorus, William Wilberforce and the abolition of slavery, Dorothy Day, Uganda martyrs, Elizabeth Fry and the Quaker tradition, Mary the mother of Jesus, the Rose window of Chartres, services in education and health, Gregorian chant, Rose of Lima, Colonel Booth and the Salvation Army, Shakespeare, Celtic spirituality, Mother Teresa, Caritas, Ignatius of Loyola, Salisbury cathedral, Irenaeus of Lyons, Orthodox icons and the Bible.

Historians also remind us of the sinful shadow side of the church with the exploitation and killing of indigenous people, the witches trials and executions, the religious wars, Inquisition, violation of personal freedoms, punishment of heretics, suppression of personal liberties, clergy abuse and so on. Any sense of triumphalism about the contribution of the Christian church to the wellbeing of humanity throughout the 2000 years of its history is also tempered by a sober assessment of its communal sinfulness.

The rigidity described above refers to the church as an institutional system and its relative paralysis in effecting significant renewal of the ways the church functions as a system. When the followers of Jesus became embedded in a political system like the Roman Empire in the 4th century, there was always a danger that power structures in upholding the church as a system would tend to dictate how the teachings of Jesus about the reign of God are proclaimed. The three temptations described in the gospels (Matthew 4:1-11; Luke 4:1-13) focus on how Jesus will use his power – for self-aggrandisement or for God's glory?

Although billions of Christians throughout the ages have found solace as members of the church, more and more Christians are now searching for an alternative orthodoxy that is intelligible and real for their everyday lives. This quest for *alternative orthodoxy* in no sense implies a capitulation to scientific materialism or a dilution of essential beliefs about God's revelation in Jesus. An alternative orthodoxy articulates core Christian beliefs in a framework whose scope embraces the whole of creation. The notion of an alternative orthodoxy does not imply a series of cognitive doctrinal formulations but a living vital corpus of beliefs and practices that orientate a Christian to experience God in Christ and the Spirit within the great story of the universe. The new sciences offer exciting possibilities for new theologies to flourish.

An alternative orthodoxy will not solve the crisis in Western Christianity of itself but will be a positive starting point for fostering a credible faith/metaphysical genre within a prevailing materialistic secular culture. There is an urgent need for the church today to remove excessive doctrinal baggage that has accumulated throughout the centuries and return to the primal and dynamic vision of Jesus in the gospels.

> **By the term 'alternative orthodoxy' I mean a corpus of essential Christian beliefs which are composed and lived within the context of the evolutionary dynamism of creation. This alternate corpus of beliefs and way of life, based on scholarship and prayerful discernment, would need to be endorsed by the official teaching church.**

Unless there is a public recognition and endorsement of an alternative orthodoxy by the official teaching church there will persist a necessary culture of subterfuge and self-regulated censorship by those promoting themes in the alternative orthodoxy of the Cosmic Christian Story. An alternative orthodoxy will never flourish if it has to be camouflaged by faux conformity.

Our cultural mores make us suspicious of words and rhetoric spoken by public figures. There is diminished attention in Christian circles to articulating right doctrines. Before the Reformation, 'orthodoxy' meant "right ways of worship'. After the Reformation, 'orthodoxy' meant 'right beliefs'. There seems less insistence today about having the 'right' beliefs. In our contemporary world, there is a general movement from concerns about orthodoxy (right beliefs) to the touch point of orthopraxis (right practice). A religious faith is more credible with actions for justice rather than words about justice. Witness rather than rhetoric carries the day in authenticating the Jesus story. There is a perceptible shift in Christian thinking that is moving from concerns about beliefs in Christ to living a Christ life, a movement from an outer to an inner Christianity. Faith is not simply an assent to a series of doctrines but a response to invitations for intimacy with a loving God.

> *Share your perceptions of the state of religious consciousness in society now.*
> *What insights have you gleaned from conversations with young people about their views on religion?*
> *Why do you think there is now a decline in religious practice in Western countries?*

The Dilemma of Responding to Scientific Consciousness

Before we begin to discuss the dilemma of science and religion we might consider the amazing phenomena of how life came to be on our earth at all. Did life emerge on earth by sheer chance? A fluke? Good luck? Or what? How did it happen that you and I and all those beautiful species all around us actually evolved? The Anthropic Principle describes how a whole series of conditions and natural constants in the life of the universe allowed life to appear. Just imagine in the evolutionary story of the universe if there had been the slightest variation in such features as the distance of the earth to the sun, the colour of the sun, the position of our solar system in the universe, the composition of water, the earth's magnetic field, the relationship between protons and electrons and so on. The fine tuning of energy and matter played its part in the birthing of life. Is there some kind of super law that we don't know about or an act of religious faith inviting us to reverence the mystery of a Creator's mind?

Science has much to say about matters raised by the anthropic principle and scientific discourses have significant implications for the Christian story.

In today's Western culture, a scientific worldview seems to be supplanting a religious worldview. In ancient societies and for most of human history, there was no distinction between religion and other spheres of life. A religious awareness was embedded in every aspect of daily life. Even as recently as the early 20th century, a Christian ethos was assumed in the public life of Western countries. However, during the 20th century, the trend towards divesting God and religion generally from public life gathered momentum. Belief in God became an option rather than an imperative, a choice not a prescription. Christian beliefs are now more closely scrutinised by an increasingly educated population where views contrary to the Christian story are easily accessible through internet media research of Google.

According to the Franciscan theologian Ilia Delio, 'Technology has empowered religion to become an open system, and because religion has now become a new channel of life outside the institution, Christ too is emerging in new ways' (2011:143). A scientific world view which permeates the whole of Western societies can seem to offer more attractive lifestyles than those proclaimed by the Christian churches. Science confidently announces to people in a down-to-earth mode such as, 'The forest fire was so severe because...' whereas religion often seems to offer explanations that are too vague and mystical for humdrum pragmatic events of life.

There have been extraordinary developments in science, especially during the last hundred years. It is difficult to comprehend and appreciate the amazing scope of scientific advances in such a short time. For the first time in history, we now possess scientific information about the evolution of the universe. We know about our cosmic origins. Just consider fundamental discoveries in such fields as cosmology, theories of the Big Bang, quantum physics and its applications in nanoscience, genetic inheritance and DNA, energy fields, string and gravity theories, evolution of the human species, brain preservation and neuroscience. The cracking of the genetic code in the middle of the 20th century by Francis Crick and Jim Watson was one of the most important scientific discoveries in the last century.

Science has probed the workings of nature and technology has enabled us to utilise the insights of science for the betterment of our lives. We simply cannot imagine our world without computers, information technology, air travel, modern medicine, smartphones, satellites and so on. A network of digital communications links the entire financial and information world within a global entity. We are all global citizens where an instant cross fertilisation of ideas is an everyday happening. A breakthrough in addressing Alzheimer's disease is known internationally within hours of its local public announcement. Advanced global technology has raised a consciousness of the world as a single place without communication borders. We are also more aware of the shadow side of scientific advances when we are confronted with an acceleration of degradation to the biosphere (place of all life) and rapid extinction of species.

Of particular significance in the scientific cultural worldview is the recognition of an evolutionary understanding of the universe. The world, and indeed the whole of the universe, is always in a state of *becoming*, always creating. In 1859, a biologist Charles Darwin published his epoch making book, *On the Origin of Species* proposing a new scientific theory about how various species evolved through a process of mutation and 'natural selection'. Adaptation and survival are the driving impulses in the evolutionary processes.

The theory of evolution has now become a dictum in understanding the transformation of all species, including humans, in the unfolding course of history (Johnson 2014, 49 - 52). The idea of evolution is basic to any appreciation of what is happening now in views about change, economics, politics, technology, psychology and spirituality. A contemporary understanding of evolution is much broader in scope than theories about biology. Today we appreciate how the dynamics of evolution embraces every facet of human and planetary life. According to the writer Carter Phipps, 'It (evolution) is better thought of as a broad set of principles and patterns that generate novelty, change and development over time' (18).

Theories about evolution challenged traditional static religious beliefs and initially met fierce resistance from most religions although some individual religious leaders recognised the veracity of evolutionary science. Contrary to those pessimists who wring their hands about the decline of church participation related to a dominant scientific world view, an evolutionary perspective on religion opens doors of consciousness towards a new appreciation of an ongoing revelation of God in creation. In his writing about evolution, the Jesuit priest and palaeontologist Teilhard de Chardin (1881-1955) wrote, 'It (evolution) is a general condition to which all theories, all hypotheses, all systems must bow and which they must satisfy henceforth if they are to be thinkable and true. Evolution is the light which illuminates all facts, a curve that all lines must follow'. The illuminating light of evolution beckons Christians forward to a Christ filled vision of hopeful possibilities for people and the whole of the earth community. Teilhard wondered if the traditional Christian world view was expansive enough for the evolution of human consciousness in a global world. In *The Divine Milieu*, Teilhard asks, 'Is the Christ of the gospel big enough for the size of the cosmos?' Teilhard's question might well be directed to all theistic religions, 'From the perspective of the billions of galaxies in a vast universe, is your creator deity big enough or has your religion fashioned a miniature god of your own making?'

A Christian view on evolution believes that God initiated the energy of creation without setting the directions of how specific dimensions in nature were to happen. Species adapted to a variety of conditions in increasingly complex patterns over millions of years. All creation is a manifestation of God's birthing energy. The divine presence pervades everything in the universe. Chaos, random selection of species, survival of the fittest and uncertainty are all integral aspects in the unfolding story of the universe. The Belgium physical chemist Ilya Prigogine explained how disequilibrium is a necessary condition for growth to occur. In the Christian story, out of the chaos of the cross came the hope of the resurrection. An evolutionary perspective of creation opens up exciting new frontiers of knowledge. Many of the future elements in the universe are yet to be discovered. Recently scientists have discovered another 500,000 stars in the Milky Way. Modern science also generates complex ethical questions. Examples of ethical dilemmas include such challenges as the rapid advances of research in artificial intelligence (AI), brain preservation and neuroscience, all of which pose formidable moral challenges for Christian beliefs and ethics in the fields of anthropology and epistemology (how we know). Confronting theological, ethical and philosophical issues are beginning to surface in the cyborg society, especially with the making of the latest robots which are anticipated to match human intelligence by 2050. What does it mean for the Incarnation when human intelligence is conversing with socially intelligent human-like robots?

There have been many revelations of the Divine Presence to humankind throughout the thousands of years of *Homo sapiens*. A person of religious faith believes that the Universal Spirit has always been present through the ages of humankind's story. The Spirit world of indigenous tribes, the rise of the great religions such as Hinduism, Taoism, Buddhism, Judaism and Islam, are all manifestations of the Universal Spirit. In Hinduism, Kundalini ('coiled one') is considered as a divine primal energy. Through the flowering of religious and philosophical wisdoms of the Axial Age (800 BCE- 300 BCE) and the revelations of God in the Hebrew Scriptures, there emerged an era of religious consciousness that was attuned in religious readiness to the teachings of prophets such as Jesus. For Christians, God's revelation is through creation, the advent of Jesus as the Christ and the presence of the Spirit in an evolving universe.

Within the context of the apparent disconnection between contemporary Western Christianity and a scientific consciousness, how might Christianity respond more creatively to the challenges of this scientific age? If the church esteems truth, then it will utilise the insights of modern science to augment its own teachings. Faith and reason are partners, not adversaries in the quest for truth and wisdom. To some degree, both science and religion are autonomous in their spheres of human activity but whenever possible they should cooperate in dialogue and mutual respect for the good of humanity and creation.

Crucial questions for a modern Christian are: 'In the light of evolutionary science, are there alternate expressions of core Christian beliefs about God's revelation in Christ that are complementary to those beliefs of the traditional Fall/Redemption story? If so, what are features of these beliefs and what are the implications for Christian living?'

The scientific worldview is a prime mover in generating a new consciousness. I would describe 'consciousness' as the inherent human ability to make sense of ourselves and the world we live in. Consciousness is a process of self-reflection which enables us to a state of self-awareness of being ourselves.

As the scientific revolution gathered pace, people began to see the world differently. Through an enlightened consciousness we have become more aware of global issues and moral imperatives relating to such concerns as justice, feminism, social fragmentation, disparity of wealth and declining planetary health. Contemporary levels of consciousness are at very different levels than those of past times. Many of the concerns of people in rural areas of medieval England are not the concerns of people now living in high rise apartments in New York or in Kenya. The more recent scientific revolution is not just a matter of developing inventions such as cars, planes, computers, mobile phones, drones and space travel. The previous scientific views of an earth-centred rather than a heliocentric world dramatically changed the worldviews of humans. No longer is humanity the centre of the universe but instead people now recognise that they inhabit a tiny planet orbiting within an immense universe of billions of planets. For centuries, science endorsed the work of Isaac Newton (1643 – 1727) who postulated that matter was a series of separate parts and operated according to fixed laws. No longer are Newtonian cause-and-effect mechanic laws valid in the scientific relational world of quantum physics.

The certainty of 19th and early 20thcenturies science has been dramatically overturned in the 20th century. According to Richard Tarnas, 'By the end of the third decade of the twentieth century, virtually every major postulate of the earlier scientific conception had been controverted: the atoms as solid, indestructible, and separate building blocks of nature, space and time as independent absolutes, the strict causality of all phenomena, the possibility of objective observation of nature' (356). As one who struggles with trying to comprehend quantum physics, I am encouraged to read how some scientists themselves state that those who claim to understand quantum physics, in reality do not understand it at all!

The new science presents concepts that are almost impossible to comprehend by human intelligence where, for example, matter and energy are interchangeable and scientific observations and explanations affect the nature of the objects being observed. The English physicist James Hopwood Jeans (d 1946) suggested that twentieth - century physics resembled, not so much a giant predictable machine but a great thought. Another English physicist Richard Feynman (1918 – 1988) considered that the reality of the universe is actually much stranger than we think. This book can only offer a cluster of salient themes in modern science which have significant implications for proposing an alternative orthodoxy of a Cosmic Christian Story rather than attempting a compendium of modern scientific advances.

Theories about quantum physics were proposed early in the twentieth century. Quantum physics challenged the previously held mechanistic theories about predictable Newtonian laws of movement and energy. The world is not made up of a series of separate building blocks but complex interdependent interactions between clusters of energy. Quantum physics proposes theories to explain the nature and behaviour of matter and energy on the atomic and subatomic levels. Quantum physics demonstrates how apparently staid matter is actually manifestations of little bundles of energy ('quanta') moving in almost infinite fields of spaces. Heisenberg's Uncertainty Principle claimed that perceptions are changed by the very act of observation. Something can be a wave or particle depending on our observations of what is happening. Actually it is consciousness, not matter, which keeps things together in perception and meaning. Consciousness transcends the particulars of material things and gives meaning to the observer.

In the perspective of quantum physics, humans exist in a complex world of interconnected relationships within the cosmos. Such relationships are much bigger and more influential than the limited scope of relationships in spheres of human existence that we observe. Things that we experience are not separate isolated segments but actually bundles of energy connecting and interacting with other bundles of energy. In a quantum understanding of the universe, elements of the universe move in and out of us. Hence we are literally in a state of oneness with the whole of the universe. We are all part of that consciousness which is a connectedness with everything in the universe. Modern science is much more cautious about making predictions with absolute certainty. Unlike the certainty of Newtonian physics, the quantum world is fluid and unpredictable (See Cox & Cohen, 126-131).

A rapidly emerging area of applied quantum physics is nanoscience and nanotechnology. Nanoscience involves the study of materials in an ultra-small scale. Researchers work at the scale of the nanometre which is one billionth of a metre and thus are able to create seemingly impossible new technologies. Nanoscience is beginning to revolutionise modes of communications, health, medicine, energy and environmental technology. Our smartphones depend on advances in nanotechnology. When we consider the amazing series of revolutions in scientific inventions during the last hundred years, we can only speculate how new inventions will radically change our lives and our levels of consciousness in the years ahead.

For a religious believer, where is the meeting point between religion and new science? *Who do you say I am?* is a disturbing question for worshiping a cosmic Christ in the world of modern science. One might wonder if there is any convergence point at all between the two realms of human experience, religion and science, or is there a permanent divorce?

On a more positive note, modern science opens doors for dialogue with religions and spirituality generally. As we have already seen, the personal dimension of human observation now plays a more central role in shaping the identity of what is observed. The principle of interconnectedness of all things in the universe affirms a holistic appreciation of creation. Energy fields suggest explanations for beliefs about a Universal Christ whose presence and grace cross time and space. Christian theology has been very tardy is grasping the opportunities presented by modern science to review their beliefs and religious practices. Modern science, especially cosmology, quantum physics and energy fields both challenge and invite Christians to reframe the Christ story within the awesome wondrous story of the universe.

> *What are some of the challenges of reconciling science and religion? Do you consider advances in science help or hinder religion?*

The dilemma of reconciling emerging world views

When people change their assumptions about their worldviews, those of a religious faith are confronted with the prospect of revising their modes of articulating and living such beliefs. When Christians began to see the world differently, they realise that traditional pre-modern ways of expressing religious beliefs no longer make sense in this evolving world. For example, contemporary scripture studies assist us in honouring the spiritual wisdom in themes such as the virgin birth, Jesus walking on water, miracles, changing of water to wine at Cana, without being locked into literal interpretations of such passages in the Bible. Far from being a biblical denier, a contemporary educated Christian appreciates how modern science and hermeneutics (methods of interpreting the Bible) uncover and deepen the spiritual richness of scripture.

The miracle of loaves and fishes (Luke 9:10 -17) symbolises the abundance of a gracious God rather than the need to believe that the miracle was some kind of divine sleight of hand in multiplying loaves and fishes. The miracle teaches that there are plenty of resources for everybody if only people would be generous in sharing – just look at those twelve baskets of food left over after everyone had eaten! The walking on water (Matthew 14: 22-33) is not an example of divine flotation across surging waves but a dramatic reassurance of God's providential care of a fledgling persecuted community. The genre of communicating religious truths in the first century was significantly different from historical methodology today. The essential point of a miracle story is not the physical act itself but the inner faith meaning of what the miracle signified. Miracles described in the New Testament are signs that the messianic age foretold by Isaiah in the 8th century BCE have come to pass. Miracles in the New Testament also have their antecedents in miracles of the Old Testament (e.g. 2 Kings 5; Exodus 4; Exodus 16; 2 Kings 2:8 -17). For the writers of the gospels, such miracles affirm the authenticity of Jesus as the promised messiah.

In a sense, we are all pilgrims, moving forward and living. Each new invention makes irrelevant many previous ways of doing things. The new sciences, especially cosmology, genetics, evolution, energy fields and quantum physics, invite us to think differently about our place in the world. An evolutionary perspective on creation sees a general dynamic movement towards more complex forms of life. We now better appreciate how our identity as humans is intrinsically bound up with all life forms in the universe. It is a stunning realisation that I am connected with every single thing that has ever been created and evolved. An interventionist God is not 'up there' somewhere but intimately permeating the whole evolutionary process of creation. The notion of *panentheism* proposes that God is both within the dynamics of creation and as well as beyond it, both as a Presence that is characterised by the immanence of reality and the transcendence of the numinous.

An appreciation of evolutionary Christianity is a movement from a static understanding of Christianity to an emerging sense of the Divine Presence in ongoing revelation. There is no closure to God's revelation within evolutionary consciousness. For a Christian, revelation did not end with the death and resurrection of Jesus as the Christ. Given the speed of scientific and cultural change, God's revelation through Christ will assume other paradigms of belief and modes of Christian living in the 22nd century. There is a growing movement in Christianity that suggests different ways of being Christian are becoming more evident. According to the theologian Don MacGregor, there is 'an evolution of Christianity that draws on ancient understandings, but incorporates modern insights. It is also creating a path that is not exclusive, but speaks to and informs other spiritual paths' (216). If Christians take seriously *The Word was made flesh and dwelt among us* (John 1:14) then they acknowledge that Jesus, like us, was biologically descended from stardust in the amazing story of the universe. The story of the universe is unfolding not halted. After centuries of thinking the world was fragmented into separate parts, we are beginning to comprehend a wholeness of the world and this thinking discards any notion of a 'God out there'.

How does a believer retain core beliefs of her or his Christian faith and yet articulate these beliefs within new world views? Jesus proposed a model for such an enterprise: *Therefore every scribe who has been trained for the kingdom of heaven is like the master of a household who brings out of his treasure what is new and what is old* (Matthew 13:52). The scribe knows that there are ancient eternal truths (old) which must be preserved and there are emerging wisdoms (new) in the treasure chest of beliefs. The danger for Christianity now is to persist in proclaiming a corpus of beliefs that are incoherent and incompatible with proven science and framed in pre-modern outmoded cosmology. Jesus warns against assuming that very static option *No one sews a piece of unshrunk cloth on an old coat, for the patch pulls away from the cloak, and a worse tear is made. Neither is new wine put into old wineskins, otherwise the skins burst and the wine is spilled...* (Matthew 9:16 -17).

It is important to emphasise that beliefs are not to be understood as abstract doctrinal propositions but pointers to ways of being religious. According to the theologian Adrian B. Smith (d 2011), 'There is no such a thing as a timeless expression of truth' (2001:6). The British monk Pelagius (354 - 418) expressed succinctly the difficulty of explicating church teachings, 'You will realise that doctrines are inventions of the human mind, as it tried to penetrate the mystery of God. You will realise that scripture itself as the work of human minds recording the example of teaching of Jesus. Thus it is not what you believe that matters - it is how you respond with your heart and your actions. It is not believing in Christ that matters - it is becoming like him' (Quoted by Newell, 11-12).

Beliefs about Jesus as the Christ orientate the Christian towards living out the gospel in everyday life. Doctrines are not set in concrete time-bound constructs but expressions of orientating a believer towards a religious truth. Every religious tradition needs a corpus of beliefs otherwise the tradition dissolves into an amorphous know-nothing. Carl Jung's warning is salutary about those who wish to dismiss doctrines in religions. Jung writes, 'Only heedless fools will wish to destroy (dogma), the lover of souls, never' (Collected Works, XI 105). A difficulty with a corpus of beliefs happens when the articulation of the beliefs become an end in itself and not a pathway into the divine mystery. A faith response to the Christian story is ultimately a response of the heart, not simply the mind. It is no coincidence that popular devotions such as the Sacred Heart of Jesus and Immaculate Heart of Mary portray an image of the heart as the icon of God's love.

The scholar Emeritus Professor Charles Taylor, in his book *A Secular Age*, writes about 'seekers' and 'dwellers' in the religious groups. 'Dwellers' stay with their inherited tradition and are content to remain there. 'Seekers' are restless in their tradition and seek an enriched faith journey according to new ideas and new life experiences. 'Seekers' are insistent that their religious faith connects with the realities of their lives and the world around them. In the internet and global world, research suggests that more and more Christians are 'Seekers' rather than 'Dwellers'.

A contrary movement to the 'Seekers' is the emergence of a new fundamentalism. The speed of cultural change seems to have generated the rise of a fundamentalism which steadfastly clings to the securities of past beliefs. Wahhabism and Salafi jihadism foster extreme beliefs as a major influences on Islam today; ultra-Orthodox Jews are a political force to be reckoned with in the Knesset of Israel; fundamentalist evangelical Christians determine the fate of politicians in some USA states and conservative voices in the Catholic church demand loyalty to *Humanae Vitae* and prohibition against women's ordination. In contrast to the dogmatism of fundamentalism, we observe how many people have quietly put aside questions about God and simply settle for making the best of life as it is now with their everyday questions. In a secular age, theocentricity (the divine as the central energy) has been largely replaced by anthropocentricity (humans the centre of energy). The proliferation of 'selfies' is a visible sign of a growing narcissist culture of anthropocentricity.

To shift one's consciousness to another way of thinking and believing, people need support, explanations and encouragement. Any dismantling of people's frame of beliefs without helping them develop meaningful ways of relating to their world and their religious faith can lead to confusion, anger and, for others, atheism or fundamentalism. Over the years of conference presenting I have sometimes encountered furious reactions from people whose faith building blocks seem to be eroded. On other occasions, people have expressed real joy at new religious insights. The reframing of a religious worldview is helped and energised by an openness to know and experience God more deeply.

> *What is your opinion about the concept of 'seekers' and 'dwellers' in the church today?*
> *Who are these people and to which group are you most sympathetic? Why?*
> *Why does it appear that there is a growth in those who might be regarded as 'seekers'?*

The dilemma of how doctrinal truths are communicated

God is always mediated through a cultural lens. Ideas about God are articulated in language modes and symbols of particular eras. Doctrines are not ends in themselves. Creedal statements are like signposts pointing to the mystery of encountering the Holy One. Beliefs are doors, not closed rooms which lead one to experience the mysterious God of love. We are not graced by God through articulating abstract formulas about God. The demand for having the right words for doctrines easily degenerates into a form of idolatry. History is replete with a host of terrifying instances of people who professed orthodox beliefs of their religion while they brutally murdered and raped in the name of their own deity. If people remain at the level of doctrinal words in living a faith life, they will never encounter the Mystery that is beyond words. Faith is trust in a living God. According to the religious writer David Tacey, those who insist that Christians should cling to a traditional way of expressing their beliefs will end up overseeing the demise of their tradition (12).

Jesus taught and lived a WAY of life, not expounded a series of doctrines. His teachings and parables proposed that we should find God where God resides in everyday life: *Consider the lilies, how they grow: they neither toil nor spin; yet I tell you, even Solomon in all his glory was not clothed like one of these* (Luke 12:27). Look around you, he exhorted his listeners, and the reign of God is right there where you are standing. It is instructive to note that when asked by the disciples of John the Baptist to say who he was, Jesus described his identity in terms of his healing mission to the afflicted: Jesus answered them, '*Go and tell John what you hear and see: the blind receive their sight, the lame walk, the lepers are cleansed, the deaf hear, he dead are raised, and the poor have good news brought to them*' (Matthew

11: 4-5). This quote is highly significant in our reflection on seeking to tell and live the Christian story in this time of consciousness. Note, Jesus did not respond to the question of his identity with titles such as, 'Saviour of the world', 'King of kings', 'Lord of the heavens'. His identity and mission are about healing and bringing people to 'life in abundance' (John 10:10). The sign of God's presence in Jesus is the transformation of people into new life and wholeness. Orthopraxis (the <u>doing</u> of the gospel, not the talking about it) is more credible in today's religious climate than orthodoxy: *Thus you will know them by their fruits* (Matthew 7:20).

For historical reasons, the early church soon began to clarify its doctrines within a great diversity of beliefs among various churches especially those beliefs relating to Christology. For the impelling reasons of political unity in the Roman Empire, especially in the fourth century, in a series of church councils such as Nicaea (325 CE) and Constantinople (381 CE), Christian orthodoxy was gradually formulated and enforced. The first executions of Christians by Christians for heresy happened in 386 CE. The bitter sectarian struggles in the time of the Reformation (16th century onwards) intensified the commitment by various Christian groups to having the correct (sic) doctrines. Christians killed one another for contrary beliefs about doctrines. Only within the last hundred years have the great majority of Christians learned to live cooperatively with diversity of beliefs. In contemporary Islam, this level of tolerance is yet to be fully realised. Even today there is unanimous opinion in Islamic jurisprudence that apostasy laws in Islam still do not permit Muslims to convert to other religions.

An increasingly educated Christian population in the West now tends to hold a more tentative affiliation with the institutional church or permanently depart from it. Research indicates that a majority of Western Christians are not hesitant in critiquing both the doctrines and modus operandi of how the church functions as a system. The rapid increment in the number of theologians who are lay and not clerics (above 70%) orientates modern theology more towards global issues rather than internal church matters. Disputes about specific doctrinal issues seem to lose their relevance in the face of immediate concerns about planetary health, terrorism, asylum seekers, job security, global poverty, economics and social media. The balance in spiritual matters between transcendence and immanence is more and more tilted towards immanence, that is, with the here-and-now of everyday life rather than the transcendence of the spiritual and mystical.

That 20,000 children die each day from drinking cholera-invested water and disease is really much more important than defending the doctrine of transubstantiation.

There is a general prevailing social distrust of public institutions, including the church. Public disclosures on sexual abuse and cover-ups by the church have shredded the role of the church as a moral leader although Pope Francis is a credible and hopeful world voice for justice and compassion. This sense of distrust of church as institution tends to motivate many Western Christians to find their own spiritual paths elsewhere. The most eminent Catholic theologian of the last hundred years, the Jesuit Karl Rahner, in his essay 'The Spirituality of the Church of the Future' wrote, 'The Christian of the future will be a mystic or will not be a Christian anymore'. Mystics aspire to encounter God directly and without intermediaries. Because the institutional church cannot control the religious experience of mystics, mysticism is viewed with cautious suspicion by the official church. History amply illustrates how often this suspicion turned into exclusion. Many of the mystics, such as Meister Eckhart (1260 - 1327) and Hildegard of Bingen (1098 -1179) who are heroines and heroes in the church story, only received acclamation centuries after their deaths.

A deeper question for those professing Christianity is perhaps not about specific doctrinal beliefs but about a sense of the ultimate meaning in life. 'What is the purpose of my life?' is an enduring question that reaches across all age groups. There is a discernible trend in contemporary spirituality which goes beyond the boundaries of institutional religions. This genre of spirituality seems to integrate the wisdoms of diverse religious traditions with the life-enhancing energies of the secular world. Questions such as the following are implicit in many aspects of conversations and wonderings: 'I know that one day I will die so what does life mean for me now?' 'Is there any way of life, such as Christianity, which can help me discover a meaning to live?' 'If there is a merciful God, why is there so much suffering and evil in the world?' 'Can the downward trend in ecological health of the earth be reversed?', 'I'm quite keen on spiritual matters but I'm not really interested in religion'. In today's world, concerns such as the threat of terrorism, financial chaos, the impact of climate change, unemployment, divisions in religion, and, for at least one third of the world's population, people's very survival, generate anxiety. There are currently sixty-five million refugees just surviving in desperate situations.

At the beginning of the twentieth century the philosopher Friedrich Nietzsche in a prophetic parable wrote about a madman who lit a lantern and walked through a market place looking for God. 'Where is God?' he kept crying out. The townsfolk mocked him for being so stupid. Finally, the madman threw down the lantern which shattered. He then cried out, 'God is dead and we have killed him'. When we think about the horrors that were to descend on Europe less than ten years after this 'God is dead' proclamation of Nietzsche in the form of the carnage of the First World War, a new dawning of the twentieth century with its technology, atomic bomb, world wars, globalisation and space travel, all these and many other momentous happenings, ensured that the 'old sky god' was dead indeed. There are no resurrections for that kind of god.

Are religions courageous enough to proclaim a new image of God within a developing cosmic consciousness? Does the church want to be anchored in safe harbours of doctrinal security even while the cultural tide is ebbing away or will the church heed the warning of Thomas Aquinas (d 1274) about renewal paralysis, 'If the highest aim of the captain were to preserve his ship, he would keep his ship in port forever'.

It would seem that one issue in the West for Christians is the question of credibility of its beliefs. The biologist Richard Dawkins and like-minded peers have a hey-day in mocking certain religious beliefs although their understandings of these beliefs are limited by their assumption that the only reality is scientific reality. They often confuse excesses in religions with the essence of religion itself and seem incapable of relating to the metaphysical dimensions of our humanity. Notwithstanding this ignorance, caricature of religion by an anti-religious movement is very popular in the social media. The public mission of the churches has also been seriously compromised by the findings of government commissions on sexual abuse in various countries and cover-ups within a closed culture of clericalism. As a consequence of these very public media exposures on sexual abuse, it will probably take a generation for the churches to restore their credibility to speak authentically on moral issues.

Over the years of my teaching aspects of Christianity, I often encounter questions about topics such as the existence of a God, the rationale for suffering, virgin birth, miracle stories in the gospels, Jesus walking on water, original sin, people sent to everlasting punishment in hell, homosexuality as an 'intrinsic disorder', infallibility of the pope, belief in God, sexual morality, women and church, miracles and so on. A critical question concerns the veracity of the Bible. The question, 'Is the Bible true?' raises all kinds of issues about the credibility of church teachings and how we understand the way the Bible was composed. Even on simple topics such as the Holy Family, traditionally imaged in art as Mary, Joseph and Jesus, a few participants at a recent conference were surprised when I remarked as an aside that the gospel of Mark names the family of Mary and Joseph as having seven children (Mark 6:3). In my travelling ministry of many years across several countries, it is a constant source of amazement to me how little of the previous hundred years of biblical scholarship and modern theology have actually filtered down to the pews. The church has a dismal record on fostering adult life and faith development. One can only wonder about the openness of seminary formation to the accumulated religious wisdoms or are seminarians still being schooled in theology that belongs to a past era of a pre-modern outmoded cosmology?

How credible are the expressions of Christian belief in contemporary consciousness? Are Christian beliefs compatible with the tenets of modern science? In a world shaped by science and insights arising out of cosmology, palaeontology, psychology, genetics and evolutionary science, do expressions of Christian belief have credibility? How do Christians respond to ethical questions raised by LGBT (lesbian, gay, bisexual and transgender)? If proven science contradicts a religious doctrine, is a Christian obliged to uphold the doctrine? How seriously should Catholics support the notion of infallibility when historians describe this doctrine as a very late arrival in the history of the Catholic Church?

Research in USA indicates that at least 30% of Christians hold a fundamentalist interpretation of the Bible. A survey of doctors in USA found that 11% of Catholic doctors and 35% of Protestant doctors held that God created humans exactly as they appear now (Roughgarden: 8). To believe literally the flood story and Noah's ark (Genesis 6 -8) necessitates a suspension of common sense. When the flood waters which covered the whole earth (sic) subsided, where did all the water go? Should Christians be resigned to function in two irreconcilable worlds, the world of science and the world of religious belief? How comfortable are Christians living their faith life with all the paradoxes of issues related to institutional church? For how much longer are Christians prepared to accept the subordination of women and subservient role of the laity in church governance? Do Christians experience their faith life as adults or as children? What can be done to better support those whom Bishop John Selby Spong calls 'believers in exile' (Spong:1999)?

> *What is the greatest problem for the church in communicating its teachings?*
> *Share some of your own experiences about the learning of doctrines in your childhood years.*
> *Discuss some ways in which the Good news has been (or is now) communicated and shared.*

The dilemma of the church as a system – is it an open or closed system?

If the Christian community is to transform humanity through the Christ power of love then the Christian community must be open to where the Spirit is present in creation. An alternative orthodoxy will never be birthed in a closed church system.

Is the church an OPEN or CLOSED system?

An OPEN church as Christian community is characterised by a culture of listening, learning, observing, discerning, praying, depthing the tradition and dialogue. An OPEN Christian community is focused on promoting the essential mission of the Good News. An OPEN Christian community encourages conversations between diverse voices in the wider community and is alert to where the Spirit is moving in world consciousness. Leaders in an OPEN system empower members of the community to share their birth gifts, their wisdoms, their passion for justice and connectedness with creation.

A CLOSED church is characterised by a culture that is rigid, resistant to change, utilising authority power to uphold structures, fixed order and excluding prophetic voices.(Ilia Delio 2011:141). A CLOSED church has lost the power of imagining a creative future for its mission except within prescribed boundaries of a designated inflexible order. A CLOSED church ignores or eschews its cultural environment.

> *Do you consider your church an 'open' or 'closed' system? Support your choice by examples from your experiences of church and from history.*
> *How might a 'closed' church system become an 'open' church system?*

The dilemma of naming the impulse point for Christian beliefs

A key issue about how Christian beliefs are articulated is the response to the following question:

What is the STARTING POINT for telling and living the Christ story?

Is the STARTING POINT for the Christ story an act of primal sin that perverted God's original plan and hence shaped the need for the restoration of humankind into God's friendship through the sacrificial death of Jesus?

or

Is the STARTING POINT for the Christ story embedded within the great evolutionary story of the creation of the universe?

What is your response to the two 'starting points' that are stated above?

How might Christians reconcile the two 'starting points' or do they need to be reconciled?

To examine this question, I will begin by outlining key elements in telling the Christ experience in the traditional way for billions of Christians throughout the ages. The Fall/Redemption Traditional Christian Story has been and is today the preeminent narrative for most Christians. Given the Jewish religious context of how the Jesus story was told in the New Testament, the language of the liturgy is understandingly replete with themes of redemption, sacrifice, atonement, sin, forgiveness, covenant, reparation and mercy. To illustrate the prevalence of the sacrificial language of the Fall/Redemption Traditional Story, consider how one of the descriptions of the Eucharist or Lord's Supper is stated in the *Catechism of the Catholic Church:* 'The *Holy Sacrifice*, because it makes present the one sacrifice of Christ the Saviour and includes the Church's offering. The terms, *holy sacrifice of the Mass, sacrifice of praise, spiritual sacrifice, pure and holy sacrifice* are also used, since it completes all the sacrifices of the Old Covenant' (n 1330). In the Fall/Redemption Traditional Christian Story the cosmic dimensions of the Incarnation (John 1:14) were gradually lost or at least marginalised after the thirteenth century. Theology and spirituality about the Incarnation rapidly became historically focused on the human condition of sin, redemption, salvation, the Last Things and grace. The Christology which developed in the early church became more orientated towards the redemptive act of Jesus for the sake of humanity rather than his preaching about the inauguration of the reign of God. The church's liturgy today is still basically influenced by medieval theology, a theology for a very different world from ours today.

This Fall/Redemption Traditional Christian Story is a foundational narrative for Christians and possibly will always remain so. I propose that the Christian community is now being invited to experience their discipleship within the vision of a new story, the Cosmic Christian Story, which resonates with an evolutionary understanding of the universe and a reconnection with the natural world. In the Fall/Redemption tradition, a Christian could go through life without any significant reference to the natural world. In the Cosmic Christian Story, the natural world is an integral feature of one's theology and spirituality.

At this juncture, I wish to divert from the theme being discussed to clarify the term 'Jesus as the Christ'. In popular writings, the term 'Jesus Christ' is often used as if 'Christ' were a kind of surname for Jesus. Jesus is the name of the person who was born in Palestine in about 4 BCE. 'Christ' ('the anointed one') is the name given by early Christians to the resurrected Jesus as the Christ. In Christian belief, Jesus is both divine and human. Christ refers to the eternal manifestation of God's presence in creation. In other religious traditions such as Hinduism, the god Krishna would represent in some mode the universal human/divine manifestation.

The debate among scholars about the relationship between the names 'Jesus' and 'Christ' is a complex topic that is a source of confusion for Christians in the pews. The interfaith theologian Ramon Panikkar (1918 -2010) explained that Jesus was the 'Christ' but 'Christ' is more universal than Jesus. As a prophetic preacher, Jesus went about teaching about the reign of God and how to follow a way of life that was in accord with God's will. Early Christianity was called 'the Way'. Within twenty years after his death and resurrection, Paul's writings were presenting Jesus as 'Christos', 'the Anointed One' who is an intermediary between God in heaven and people on earth (Morwood: 60 -69). It is impossible to do justice to this topic in a book of this brevity except to acknowledge the contrasting views among scriptural scholars as to whether the Pauline Christ is compatible with the portrayal of the prophetic teacher Jesus of the gospels. It was Paul who took the gospel to the wider Gentile world. An element in the confusion about Paul's Christology is how he modified his teachings to different cultural environment such as a Jewish flavour to the Christians in

Rome, and a Greek mystery religion flavour to other communities such as Christians in Corinth.

> *Share some insights from reading this chapter about a series of dilemmas?*
> *Which dilemma(s) is (are) most relevant to your Christian faith today?*
> *Which dilemma would you like to know more about?*

Conclusion

This chapter has considered some of the dilemmas of the Christian community in its mission to communicate the Good News of the gospel and give witness to its values for life.

The next chapter describes four contextual issues that have bearing on discussing the main belief features in the Fall/Redemption Traditional Christian Story.

Chapter Two

Context issues in the Traditional Christian Story

All things evolve in this world. It is a principle of life. Cultures and societies evolve as well, and the expressions of all religions change as societies change. There are many questions in today's society that are not addressed within traditional Christianity, and many issues that need to be looked at again in the light of discoveries and realizations within the last one hundred and fifty years. In the Western world, huge numbers of people have walked away from the traditional, doctrinal, overarching story offered by the institutional Christian Church – and that is very sad as it actually has so much to offer if only it could escape from its straightjacket of doctrine and liturgy.

MacGregor, D. *Blue Sky God: The Evolution of Science and Christianity*, 7.

Before we describe salient features of the Fall/Redemption Tradition, four significant issues need to be addressed. All four issues have direct bearing on the theme of this book. The four issues offer a framework for a critique of the Traditional Christian Story and access to an appreciation of the Cosmic Christian Story.

The four issues are as follows:

- the relationship between *mythos* and *logos*;
- the role of imagination in religious discourse;
- the meaning of 'paradigm shifts';
- the Jewish context of the New Testament.

Mythos/logos

A critically important aspect of religions generally is to clarify how people relate to their religions in two basic ways. Scholars name these two ways as *mythos* and *logos* (Armstrong 2000, xv). Each way of thinking and articulating beliefs has its own mode of expressing religious wisdom. Both *mythos* and *logos* are essential for the articulation of religious beliefs and practices.

Confusion between understanding *mythos* and *logos* in religions generates perplexity, rationalism and fundamentalism. If people read myths are literal stories, they not only miss the wisdom of the myth but all too readily dismiss the myth as some impossible to believe fairytale.

Mythos offers people a deep meaning story which taps into archetypes and eternal truths. Myth is not concerned with practical matters of worship, doctrines and religious structures. Myth provides people with enduring stories to live by and is often expressed in symbolic language (see Tacey: *Beyond Literal Belief: Religion as Metaphor*).

Logos is the practical manifestation of a religion. *Logos* enables people to practise their religious beliefs through formulating a belief system, articulating doctrines and developing religious structures and worship. *Logos* is pragmatic and rational.

Both *mythos* and *logos* are essential and complementary for a holistic participation in religion.

Religion without *mythos* is reduced to a form of beliefs and rituals without an inner captivating sacred story.

Religion without *logos* is reduced to an amorphous story removed from external realities and practices of faith.

Let me illustrate this topic with a story from my own travels.

On one of my pilgrimages to Israel, I climbed the hill on the outskirts of Jerusalem to the Mount of the Ascension. A guide asked if I was a Christian and if so, did I wish to see how Jesus ascended to heaven. 'Long way to heaven, sir. Christ need very big jump to get up there', he said, pointing to the blue sky above us. The invitation was too good to miss. The guide, a very athletic fellow, set off running across the hill and then took impressive leaps into the air. After a series of running and leaping demonstrations, he then called me over to show me the indention in the rock where supposedly the heel of Jesus had dug when he took off with a massive jump into the heavens (sic) above us. I gladly gave him the money he asked for but refrained from any discussion about the *mythos* and *logos* of the ascension story.

Share your experiences of how 'mythos' and 'logos' have been understood in your faith development.

Imagination

Imagination is the gift to move us beyond our perceived realities and reconstruct new images and symbols. Imagination is nature's gift to us to envisage what might be. Through imagination we can dream of a world without wars, people with adequate food and interreligious cooperation. Religious imagination empowers us to other transformative possibilities and other visions, including visions about the nature of God and a lifestyle energised by the Dream of Jesus, the reign of God. Through imagination, the Christian community can envision a collaborative style of church governance. Might we not let our imagination soar and imagine every single person on the planet living in harmony within the network of life in creation and having enough food for each day?

At an intellectual level, God is unknowable. We recall the words of St Augustine (354 - 430) 'If you understand him, he is not God' (*Sermon* 117.5). The unknown 14th century author of *The Cloud of Unknowing* wrote, 'Even if a man is deeply versed in the understanding and knowledge of all spiritual things ever created, he can never, by such understanding come to know an uncreated spiritual thing'. Thomas Aquinas expressed this mystery of God's unknown character: 'Hence in the last resort all that man knows of God is to know that he does not know him, since he knows that what God is surpasses all that we can understand of him'(*De Potentia*, q, 7, a.5. ad.14). The metaphor of God as Trinity expresses something of the mystery within the entire universe where there is an underlying oneness or unity in all of creation.

Nature has its own laws about this unifying power which we are only beginning now to understand. The physicist David Bohm (1917–1992) expresses the unifying energy in all forms of life through his concept of 'implicate order'. The theory of 'implicate order' is a deeper and fundamental order of reality describing the essential unity of all things. However, within this oneness, there is also an amazing diversity of life forms. The whole of nature is a series of interacting energies. Species appear and disappear. Not only did the dinosaurs become extinct 65 million years ago but also fresh water sharks. Mammals lost 35% of their species. The dynamic interchange of cells and organisms is formed, breaks down and reforms in continuous motion. All of creation is in one sense a trinity of relationships, whole yet diverse, one yet many. One can only gaze in awe at the ingenuity of the divine imagination in creation. Complexity in evolution is a model for the metaphor of God as Trinity.

We articulate words about God describing the nature of God with the metaphor of Trinity. Perhaps only through imagination can we envision something of God through imagining God as a communion of love. To seek to intellectualise the paradox of God as Trinity is a forlorn exercise.

Mathematics of threes and ones will never solve our understanding of the Trinity. There are many streams which flow into the river of Trinitarian love. Possibly only through imagination can we grasp something of the nature of the mystery of an intimate God. God as Trinity is an imaginative construct to remind us that we cannot live in isolation but exist within a relational earth community which is ever growing and changing. God as Trinity is within all things and beyond all things. The very notion of God as Trinity is more in the realm of poetry, art and music rather than a theological intellectual concept. Other religions have triune deities such as Vishnu, Shiva and Shakti in Hinduism. An Egyptian cult worshipped Isis and Serapis with the divine child Horus.

In ancient times, religions expressed their core beliefs in symbolic language of sacred myths. Through imaginative stories, tribes connected their world with the divine spirits around them in nature. Origin stories and creation myths sought to give cultural meaning to the rhythms of nature and mysteries of life. Ancient peoples asked, 'What is our relationship to the moon, sun, stars, wind and earth?', 'Where did we come from?', 'Why do we exist?' They composed sacred myths to explain these mysteries of life and give their tribe a communal identity.

One such sacred myth is told in the opening chapters of Genesis (Chapter 1-3) about the creation of the world, the first humans and their first disobedience. In the writings of the New Testament, the sacred myth of the Fall provided the theological context for the meaning of the life, mission, death and resurrection of Jesus as the Christ. Actually there is no such happening as a 'Fall' in a Jewish understanding of the creation myth. A problem always occurs in religion when a sacred myth is taken literally. When literalism supplants a mythical genre of a sacred story, the power of the myth is lost or distorted.

There is an urgent need to REIMAGINE our theological assumptions about Christ in the light of a cosmic vision, to re-imagine the form and language of liturgy and a trans-religious spirituality. Why not re-imagine a Profession of Belief rather than recite the Nicene Creed which arose out of disputations with Arius in the 4th century? Worshipers at Eucharist are aware that the Nicene Creed says nothing about the teachings of Jesus which surely should be an essential item in any Christian profession of faith. Why not re-imagine the celebration of a participatory Lord's Supper? When will Christians begin to read the scriptures and worship through the imaginative eyes of a wondrous creation? Christians need to re-imagine a new framework for theological thinking outside the Greek philosophical framework - a new theological framework whose foundation is the magnificent cosmic story of the universe.

Jesus invited, urged and challenged his listeners to re-imagine different ways of being religious where God is *Abba*, where the exemplar of compassion is the hated Samaritan (Luke 10: 25-37), where the first witnesses to the resurrection are women (Matthew 28:1-8), where the Beatitudes announce a series of blessings through a compilation of paradoxes: *Blessed are the poor in spirit, for theirs is the kingdom of heaven. Blessed are those who mourn, for they will be comforted. Blessed are the meek, for they will inherit the earth* (Matthew 5:3-5). Why not share a Dream like the reign of God Dream of Jesus? How could an abandoned crucified prophet be the promised Messiah and be raised up by God as the Christ? Is our image of God too comfortable and predictable? Jesus held up the child's gift of imagination as an ideal for conversion: *Truly I tell you, unless you change and become like children, you will never enter the kingdom of heaven* (Matthew 18:3).

Our world of social media is awash with images but these images are often packaged by global corporate consumerism. Our minds are anesthetised by the numbing influences of mechanistic rationalism. A closed church system is fearful of imagination lest its power base is threatened. How might discernment and creative imagination make accessible to us images that are life-enhancing for people and creation? Let the artists, musicians and poets lead us into realms of beauty and possibilities. Why be imprisoned by cell bars of prescribed realities when imagination is the key to unlock our predictable prisons to new dreams? Let the divine imagination of creation evoke awe and wonder, leading us to worship a cosmic Christ.

Share some of your imaginations about a different world and a different church?

Paradigm shifts

Every so often in history, there is a significant 'shift' in communal thinking that changes the ways people live and act. Thomas S. Kuhn in 1970 called this phenomenon a 'paradigm shift'. Kuhn described this shift as 'the constellation of beliefs, values, techniques and so on shared by the members of a given community' (Kuhn. T.S. *The Structure of Scientific Revolutions.*

2nd. With a postscript [Chicago 1970] 175. The scripture scholar Marcus Borg defined a paradigm as, 'A paradigm is *a comprehensive way of seeing*, a way of seeing a *"whole"'* (4).

Perhaps the most famous of all paradigm shifts was the shift from an earth-centred universe to a heliocentric model of the universe. For 1500 years, the Ptolemaic paradigm dominated the scientific and religious view of earth in relation to the sun. Copernicus proposed that planets move around the sun not the earth. The work of Nicolaus Copernicus (1473 -1543) and verified by Johannes Kepler (1571-1630) turned traditional biblical views of the world upside down. The paradigm shift to a heliocentric universe was further demonstrated by the astronomical investigations of Galileo Galilei (1564 -1642). The opposition of the churches to this new physics severely discredited the church in the eyes of scientists who perceived ecclesiastical repression as an enemy of science.

History has shown that science won the day. Only during the last seventy years has there been a cautious reconciliation between science and religion. The paradigm shift from an earth-centred to a heliocentric universe was much more than a shift in theories of physics and cosmology but a whole new radical understanding of humans in the expanse of a vast universe. Our destiny is woven into the intricate web of life of everything in the universe. A paradigm shift in understanding the human place in the world raises fundamental questions about the meaning of the Incarnation within the dynamics of creation. The story of the Incarnation cannot be separated from the cosmic story.

A further example of a paradigm shift which had far reaching consequences in Judaism related to the role of the temple in Jewish life. A major paradigm shift in Judaism happened when the First and Second temples were destroyed (587 BCE and 70 CE). After almost 1000 years of temple worship as the convergence point for Jewish liturgy and religious life, the temple was no more. After the Roman demolition of the temple (70 CE) some Jewish writers wondered if Judaism itself had lost its spiritual core. Judaism faced a major challenge to its very existence with the destruction of its unifying cultic centre and having no further access to sacrificial worship. However, within a short time after the Second Temple destruction, rabbinic literature created a new paradigm of Jewish religious expressions. Instead of the temple at Jerusalem, the synagogue became the gathering place for Jews at worship.

The Bible urges us to 'repent'. Most people interpret the call to repentance as a call to conversion, a call to turn away from sin. The Greek word for 'repent' is *metanoia* which means literally 'go beyond the mind' (*meta* 'beyond' and *noia* 'mind'), that is, move to a new paradigm of experiencing with a gracious God. A follower of Jesus is confronted with the disturbing paradigm: *But many who are first will be last, and the last will be first* (Matthew 20:30). This radical injunction from Jesus turns upside down many of our assumed suppositions about our religious beliefs and even those of faith itself.

The scientist Albert Einstein once remarked that it was impossible to solve a problem with the same mindset that created the problem.

To move from living a Christian faith within the Traditional Christian Story to being Christian within a complementary Cosmic Christian Story invites a believer into a paradigm shift in consciousness.

Share some significant paradigm shifts in your own faith and life journey?

Jewish context of the New Testament

The writings of the New Testament are almost unintelligible without an appreciation of their Jewish context. In the gospels, we read how Jesus went to the Feast of Dedication (Hanukkah), the Day of Atonement (Yom Kippur – Leviticus 16:16 and 16:30) and the Feast of the Tabernacles (Sukkot). All the New Testament writers were Jews. The first fifty years of what later became known as Christianity conducted worship within the rituals of first century Judaism and the life of the synagogue. The later feasts of the church were influenced by the Jewish liturgical calendar especially by the Jewish feasts of Passover, Hanukkah, Yom Kippur and the harvest feast of Sukkoth. To better know Jesus, Christians are encouraged to deepen their understanding of the Jewish Jesus.

In the New Testament, the Traditional Christian Story was composed by followers of Jesus who were steeped in their Jewish faith and Jewish liturgical rituals. The writers of the New Testament could only express their experience of Jesus in thought patters of their own time and religious consciousness. The enterprise of reframing the Christian story from a Traditional Christian Story to a Cosmic Christian Story assumes an awareness of the Jewish roots of the Traditional Christian Story where temple blood sacrifice and covenant fidelity played a critical role in Jewish worship and devotions. The holiest day in Judaism is the feast of Yom Kippur meaning 'Day of Atonement' celebrating a day set aside for making atonement for the sins of the past year (Leviticus 23:26 -32).

Christian liturgy is replete with references to, 'washing away sins through the blood of Christ', 'lamb of God who takes away the sins of the world', 'an unbloody sacrifice', 'a new covenant' and so on. There are difficulties in appreciating the depth of New Testament writings without some knowledge of Jewish life and worship in first century Palestine. Only recently have there been serious studies by Christians of the Jewish Jesus. Perhaps a growing historical awareness of the heritage of vicious anti-Semitism and the unspeakable horror of the Holocaust (Shoah) has jolted Christians into recovering the Jewish roots in their Christian faith.

A better understanding of the Jewish framework for interpreting God's revelation in Jesus is helpful in exploring features of an alternative Cosmic Christian Story whose framework is the story of the universe.

Share your levels of knowledge about Judaism and discuss how this knowledge (or lack of it) has influenced your Christian faith?

> *Which of the four context issues described in this chapter is most relevant to your own religious development?*
> *Which context issue would you like to know more about?*

Conclusion

The four themes described above are all relevant for discussing the topic of comparing the complementary genres of the Traditional Christian Story and the Cosmic Christian Story.

Let us now turn to describe the main features of the Traditional Christian Story.

Chapter Three

The Fall/Redemption Traditional Christian Story

It is in the light of our emerging world view that we are led to reconsider what we mean by 'the Christ', especially in relation to the person of Jesus of Nazareth. Of all the factors composing our world view that are causing Christians to rethink their notion of Christ, I suggest that the predominant factor is our present understanding of evolution. Whether or not we accept the manner of its happening as proposed by Darwin – by the survival of the fittest – the fact of evolution of our species is now more than a hypothesis. It has caused our world view to change from the static to the dynamic; everything is continually in a process of change. Ideas, theories, doctrines, beliefs too are in constant process of change, no longer set in concrete for all eternity.

Smith, A. B. *God, Energy and the Field*, 2008, 69.

This chapter outlines the main features of the Traditional Christian Story and reflects on the themes in the narrative.

The following description of a dominant Fall/Redemption Traditional Christian Story highlights the main articles of beliefs throughout its two thousand years of history.

Traditional Christian story

God created the world and all things, including humans. The world of creation was good.

However, sin and disorder entered the world through the disobedience of our first parents, Adam and Eve.

By their sin, Adam and Eve were banished from the Garden of Eden and lost their primal harmony with nature. Adam and Eve and their children had to undergo death, till the soil for their livelihood and Eve to suffer pain in childbirth.

Because of the sin of Adam and Eve, all people inherited sin when they were born. This sin was called Original Sin.

Eventually God sent his Only Son Jesus, who became the Christ, to deliver us from this state of sinfulness through his life, death and resurrection.

The sacrifice of Jesus on the cross was a redeeming act to open the gates of heaven for humankind. This sacrifice of Jesus was an act of atonement to restore humankind to God's friendship.

In Christ, all people can find their salvation through his redeeming grace.

During our life, we make moral choices that determine whether we will go to heaven or hell after death.

The church, which grew out of the first community of disciples, is now entrusted with the mission of Christ to share God's grace with the faithful.

The church, through sacraments, devotions and practices for the common good, offers the faithful pathways to salvation. The hierarchy of the church exercises governance to promote the mission of the church.

Is the above description of the Traditional Christian Story in accord with your own understanding of the tradition?

Are there any modifications you wish to make to this outline of the Traditional Christian Story?

Reflections on the Traditional Christian Story

The above description of the framework for Christian belief is the basic paradigm for the Christian community. In liturgy and Christian living, the belief framework has been significantly theologically and culturally nuanced through the 2000 year old Christian story. The core themes as stated above are common to virtually every Christian church. The framework is endorsed by much of the New Testament writings, at least in the writings of the New Testament as interpreted by most Christians.

All theology is always contextualised according to its time in history, its ethnicity, religious heritage and cultural environment.

Early Christians believed that the Christ event was the fulfilment of the mission of Israel, God's Chosen people. New Testament writings about Jesus were shaped by the Hebrew scripture. These New Testament writings selected prophetic verses from the Hebrew scripture to demonstrate how Jesus was the anticipated Messiah. However, when church membership became Gentile and integrated into the Roman Empire, continuity with the people of Israel was supplanted or lost. After the fourth century, the future of Christian beliefs and governance were significantly influenced by Greek philosophy and Roman law.

As explained previously, God's revelation in Jesus happened within the context of the religious heritage of Israel with Jewish scriptures and sacrificial worship. God's revelation is always within, not beyond historical consciousness. Jesus was a Jew faithful to his Jewish heritage. New Testament writers interpreted Jesus as the Christ from their Jewish cultural and religious lens. In the aftermath of the resurrection of Jesus, New Testament writers described how Jesus fulfilled the expectations of the coming of the Messiah. Jesus as the risen Christ was the long awaited Messiah (Luke 24: 27), the Son of Man (Daniel 7:13), fulfilling the covenant (Jeremiah 31:31;) (Hebrews 8:8-13;)(Hebrews 12:24), the Expected One (Jeremiah 33:14 -16) and Suffering Servant (Isaiah 53:4 -9). Matthew and Luke rearranged historical events to ensure that Jesus was born in Bethlehem, David's city, rather than somewhere else.

Critique of the Fall/Redemption Traditional Christian Story

When we critique the narrative of the Traditional Christian Story from the perspectives of the new unitive consciousness, contemporary theology and modern science, there are a number of issues for discussion.

Those who have reservations about the summary of beliefs stated above or hold that the topic is passé are encouraged to listen attentively to the language of regular church liturgy and devotional prayers. For Catholics, a reading of *The Catechism of the Catholic Church* clearly articulates the Fall/Redemption Traditional Christian Story, especially the section Part One: The Profession of Faith. The following statement from a recent parish Easter Newsletter reflects a typical understanding of the Traditional Christian Story,

> 'Sin has many effects and consequences; none of them, however, is more terrible than our separation from God, in this life and in eternity. This was the consequence of the Sin of Adam and Eve, who were banished from the Garden, where they walked and talked with God. All humanity has shared in the sin of Adam and so we share its consequences... taking the initiative Himself, God sent his only Son to take on human flesh and to effect a wondrous reconciliation. By dying He destroyed our death and by rising He has restored our life.'

Let us consider some of these themes in the Traditional Christian Story:

1. The story begins with a problem, that is, humans have sinned and their sinfulness has alienated them from God. Hence the starting point for the Christ story is motivated by a negative event. The starting point for telling the Christ story has its origins in God's plan to rectify humanity's moral failure because of the sin of Adam and Eve (Genesis 1-3). According to a literal interpretation of the

Genesis myth, God's original plan for humans was now in disarray. The human condition, once so wholesome in the initial creation, degenerated into a state of sinfulness because of the disobedience of Adam and Eve.

2. Today we question how the literalism of the Genesis myth was utilised as a rationale for understanding the mission of Jesus. God's original plan for creation was not a failure. Jesus did not come to implement a rescue mission. For a theist (one who believes in a divine power), the creative energy of the Spirit impels creation through an evolutionary process of birth, death and rebirth.

3. The starting point of the Traditional Christian Story seems to be significantly oblivious of the 13.7 billion years before the advent of humankind. The focus of the Christ event in the Traditional Christian Story is the imperative to rectify humankind's sin. Such a focus seems to suggest that creation itself was irrelevant or at least peripheral to the core of the Christian story. The focus on the fate of humanity moved the transformation or redemption of the whole of creation to the margins of the story. In the Fall/Redemption Traditional Christian Story the earth is viewed as a temporary place where one lived for a brief time before death moved a person's soul into eternal life. Why worry about ecological concerns if the ultimate goal of life is to live, according to the words of the famous hymn 'Hail Holy Queen' (Salve Regina), 'mourning and weeping in this vale of tears'? What do Christians make of the injunction of Paul to the Philippians, *But our citizenship is in heaven, and it is from there that we are expecting a Saviour, the Lord Jesus Christ* (3:20)? During the last century, modern science has revealed the evolutionary story of the universe and our interdependence of all things in creation, thus bringing creation back into the heart of the redemptive story.

4. Adam and Eve have traditionally been regarded as real people in church teachings. Palaeontology tells us there were no such people as Adam and Eve. The human species evolved over millions of years and there were several strands of the human species long before *Homo sapiens* eventually evolved about 150,000 years ago. The characters Adam and Eve are mythical symbols for humankind. The name Adam is from the Hebrew word 'Adamah' meaning 'of the

earth'. Eve means 'mother of all living'.

5. There is no biological evidence to show that we are born morally bad (original sin). Every parent knows that her or his new born child is capable of both altruism and evil when they achieve maturity. Neuroscience confirms the experience of parents (Newberg). Our DNA is a mixture of a propensity to do both good and evil. God created the universe as an act of love and gave humans the power to make good or evil choices. We do not inherit evil when we are born. Humans are not born as a fallen race but incomplete in our self-centredness. Humanity has always been in God's Presence. Perhaps Carl Jung's concept of the 'shadow' (the unconscious negative side of our personality) might be a better explanation than the doctrine of original sin to describe the reality of personal and communal sinfulness. According to Jung the shadow is to be acknowledged and transformed into positive energy for growth (redemption).

6. The doctrine of original sin was never part of the corpus of beliefs in the first four hundred years of Christianity and is unknown in the religious traditions of Judaism and Islam (Toews: 87-89). The doctrine of original sin developed as an explanation of the reality of personal and communal sin. The articulation of the doctrine arose from the writings of Augustine (354 - 430). Scripture scholars today recognise that St Augustine used a faulty translation of Romans 5:12 to explain his doctrine of original sin. The doctrine of original sin became official church teaching in the Council of Orange (529). When the Genesis text was understood literally, that is, each person inherited sin from some purported primal sin from Adam and Eve, the essential meaning of the sacred myth about sin in the world (Genesis 3) was lost. Worse still, Christian anthropology was negatively biased towards our sinfulness. St Augustine's famous words have echoed across the centuries. In his book Enchyridion he wrote, '... So the matter stood; the dammed lump of humanity was lying prostrate, no, was wallowing in evil, it was falling headlong from one wickedness to another; and joined to the faction of the angels who had sinned, it was paying the most righteous penalty for its imperious reason'(27). The doctrine of original sin contradicted a hopeful appreciation of being human.

To critique the doctrine of original sin is obviously not to deny the pernicious impact of individual and communal sin. The harsh reality of sin as a degradation of our humanity is well attested every day in the public media and through our own self-awareness of sinfulness. The mystery of sinfulness needs to be articulated in a mode that is different from the current church teaching and cosmic in its scope. Modern theology is formulating alternative modes of expressing the propensity to sin such as 'falling upwards' in the evolutionary human development of consciousness or explaining how personal and tribal self-interest conflict with altruism. Teachings about sin explain how sinfulness is part of human experience. A problem for revising the doctrine of original sin as presently defined in church teachings is that the doctrine is intertwined with other doctrines such as the redemptive mission of Christ and salvation. It is, therefore, understandable that that there will be much resistance from the magisterium (official teaching church) for the doctrine of original sin to be reformulated. A revision of the doctrine of original sin implies a revision of how the redemptive mission of Jesus as the Christ is articulated.

7. The acceptance of the doctrine of original sin in the Western church after the 6th century affected the theology of baptism. After the validation of original sin in church doctrine, rather than appreciating baptism as essentially a sacrament of initiation into the Christian community, the emphasis on baptising became more about washing away the stain of original sin. Because of the need to remove original sin, baptism of children became standard liturgical practice. Children who died before baptism went to a place called limbo. Even as recent as seventy years ago, it was not uncommon to hear that infants in danger of death were baptised by Catholic nurses. The doctrine of Immaculate Conception arose out of teachings about original sin.

8. The doctrine of atonement taught by St Anselm of Canterbury (1033-1109) held that only One who was both divine and human could atone for the first sin because humans had offended God (*Cur Deus Homo* 1098). In medieval culture, if a person had dishonoured his lord then he had to make reparation for the fault. Since the eleventh century,

the official doctrine of the church taught that restoration from sin was the reason for the coming of Jesus as the Christ. The doctrine of atonement was affirmed as the official teaching of the church at the Council of Trent (1545 -1563). The concept of atonement is alien to modern consciousness and is a relic of medieval culture.

There are other metaphors in the New Testament to explain the reason for the death of Jesus but the atonement or satisfaction theory became embedded in Christian theology and official church teachings. Perhaps atonement might be better explained by describing the mission of Christ as 'at-one-ment', leading people to union with God. Another interesting aspect of the atonement explanation is to situate the concept within the realm of 'morphic resonance' whereby energy of the sacrifice of Jesus is transmitted through the energy waves of healing for all humanity. An explanation of the theory of 'morphic resonance' will be presented in a later chapter.

9. The very idea that God would demand a terrible death for God's Son to make restitution for sin is repulsive to modern sensibilities. God is not some kind of vengeful deity demanding a just payment for sin. Why would a loving God not simply offer forgiveness to sinful humankind? The doctrine of atonement seems to suggest that the purpose of Jesus' coming was to die in reparation for our sins and restore humanity to God's friendship.

10. The religious and social context of the New Testament writers was fashioned by the beliefs, rituals and culture of first century Judaism. Once a year, the High Priest offered sacrifice as an act of atonement for the sins of the Jewish people. For New Testament writers, Christ as the new High Priest offered a universal sacrifice. Through his death this sacrifice atoned for the sins of humankind (Hebrews 5:1-6).

11. What is the fate of the billions of people who have no relationship or interest at all with the Christian story? Are they outside the scope of salvation through Christ? If Christians insist that Christ died for everyone, how would this belief resonate with people of other religions such as Islam, Judaism, Buddhism, Hinduism, those of indigenous beliefs or those of no religious belief at all? How might the redemptive Christ be understood in a multi-faith perspective? Christians represent about 30% of the world's 7.4 billion people.

Recent theology has developed themes about a Universal or Cosmic Christ as a Sacred Divine Presence who is trans-religious and beyond specific creeds and traditions. The concept of a Universal Christ may be better appreciated by exploring the power of the Christ experience moving through energy fields by a process of morphic resonance.

12. The cycle of birth and death is integral to everything in the evolutionary created universe. The reality of death has nothing to do with a literal interpretation of the Genesis explanation that death was a consequence of a primal sin (Genesis 3:19). Death and the fragmentation of life are essential features in the evolutionary cycle of how the universe evolves. In a certain sense, suffering is a necessary ingredient of evolution. Creatures survive by feasting off other creatures. Cataclysmic disasters such as floods, earthquakes and forest fires are expressions of the ever changing patterns of evolving natural forces such as shifting of tectonic plates and dramatic climate changes.

13. The pre-modern assumptions about a three tiered universe (heaven, earth, underworld) are obsolete in the light of modern cosmology and science. For almost two thousand years, there was an almost universal belief about the fixed universe of the Greco-Egyptian astronomer Ptolemy (100 -170). In a Ptolemaic universe, the static flat earth was circled by the sun and planets. Heaven as being somewhere 'up there' and hell 'down there'. Heaven was a place where the good were rewarded. Hell was a place of eternal punishment where the wicked paid a terrible price for their evil lives. The notion of a 'Sky-God' who mysteriously is 'up-there' to direct human life has little credibility today.

14. The idea that humans are the pinnacle of creation as a literal interpretation of the sacred creation myth is an antiquated notion of human identity in creation. Humans have a unique role in creation but it is a role of kinship or companionship with all forms of life in the planet. They do not have domination over all creation (Genesis 1:28) if the nature of the domination implies irresponsible and capricious vandalism towards planetary health. Humans are very late comers to the story of the universe, perhaps only a few million

years old as hominids within a 13.7 billion expanse of creation.

15. A literal interpretation of the Genesis myth claimed that sin entered the world through the weakness of the woman Eve who succumbed to the serpent's temptation. Eve's decision reinforced prevailing Greek and Roman cultural assumptions about patriarchy and the inferior status of women. In the Yahwist strand of the Genesis myth (2:4 -3:24), the woman is a 'helper' (2:18) and clearly the weak link in the story. Such assumptions have left an enduring mark on the misogynist structures of the church. One of the early Church Fathers Tertullian (d c 200) in his work *Modesty in Apparel Becoming to Women in Memory of the Introduction of Sin into the World through a Woman*, wrote about Eve, 'You are the devil's gateway; you are the unsealer of that forbidden tree; you are the first deserter of the divine law, you are she who persuaded him whom the devil was not valiant to attack. You destroyed so easily God's image, man. On account of your desertion, even the Son of God had to die'.

16. Widespread ignorance of the language of sacred myth resulted in the formulation of Christian doctrine and biblical teachings in a literal rather than a mystical mode. Once the mythical genre of religious beliefs was lost or minimised a literal interpretation of the Bible became the accepted way of interpreting scripture. Literalism in scripture and doctrine ultimately leaves religious beliefs into a never-never land of incredibility. In *Who is Jesus? Answers to your Questions About the Historical Jesus*, the scripture scholar John Dominic Crossan wrote, 'My point, once again, is not that ancient people told literal stories and we are now smart enough to take them symbolically but they told them symbolically and we are now dumb enough to take them literally'.

17. The restorative starting point for a rationale of why Jesus became man (John 1:14) tended to reinforce a penitential spirituality which was orientated towards turning away from sin and saving one's soul. Such spirituality focused on what happened after death, that is, judgment and then heaven or hell. 'After-death' spirituality ignored or at least minimised the day-by-day human condition and ecological concerns. Penitential spirituality is uncomfortable with the notion of 'imperfect spirituality', that is, a

spirituality that is wholesome but very much a 'work in progress'. The Genesis sacred myth of creation and human origins images two basic symbols of the story of humans in creation - the Tree of Life out of which all things come and the Tree of Knowledge representing humans crossing the threshold of consciousness as *Homo sapiens*, capable of making moral decisions. The problem for Christians was not in the wisdom embedded in the sacred myth but in the literalism of interpreting the myth as a rationale for the Christ story.

Cautionary note

A series of cautions are helpful at this juncture in order to balance this critique of the Fall/Redemption Traditional Christian Story.

The above comments seem to portray a negatively orientated Christianity. The actual experiences of billions of Christians living the Fall/Redemption Traditional Christian Story for 2000 years have also been a venerable tradition of spiritual security, holiness, loving and giving in service. The Fall/Redemption Traditional Christian Story is firmly situated in the Jewish framework of the New Testament. When we reflect on the 2000 year old traditions of spirituality, worship, influence of Christian culture, music, art, services to the poor, saints, monasteries, cathedrals, ministries, devotions and so on, we are inspired by the power of the Spirit throughout the ages in energising this tradition. Christians who are content with living their Christian life within the framework of Fall/Redemption paradigm are encouraged to continue celebrating their faith according to their beliefs and devotions.

Another comment notes that during the previous fifty years, much of the harshness of the Traditional Christian Story has been softened. Rarely do we hear of homilies about the dire punishments of hell, homilies which were regular fare in my childhood days. The papacy of Pope Francis and other Christian leaders seem to be promoting a much more gentle and merciful Christianity in Christian communities. Moral theology is more orientated towards the existential situation of each person rather than simply applying punitive moral judgments according to inflexible classical moral principles of natural law.

God's revelation in the Fall/Redemption Christian Tradition is an enduring source of grace and hope for billions of Christians. Christians, including thousands of canonised saints, have drunk from deep wells of the rich spiritual heritage of the Traditional Christian Story. The Traditional Christian Story will always be a reservoir of comfort, inspiration and foundational beliefs for most Christians. The lived experiences of Christians in the Traditional Christian Story are amazingly diverse, ethnically fashioned and shaped by levels of consciousness in different historical eras.

A further cautionary observation is to recall how a cosmic appreciation of Christ is evident in some writings of Paul (cf Colossians), Irenaeus (d c 202), the Greek Fathers such as Origen (d 254) and Maximus the Confessor (580 - 662), Bonaventure (1221-1274), Hildegard of Bingen (1098 -1179) and Duns Scotus (1266 -1308). The core elements of Cosmic Christian Story discussed in the following chapters have always resided somewhere in the foundational Christian story. A creation centred Christ story was more evident in the first millennium of Christianity than in the second millennium.

The principle of sacramentality (God is present in all of creation) has always been strongly espoused in Catholic theology and spirituality. Celtic and Franciscan spiritualities are well known examples of this theological heritage. Bonaventure, a companion of Francis of Assisi (1182 -1226), preached and wrote about the intimate relationship between the Incarnation and creation as a way of understanding Christ. Eastern Orthodox theology and spirituality have generally avoided the atonement bias of Western Christianity especially in its theology of the Incarnation. The early Greek Fathers saw the Incarnation, not as an afterthought of God, but as an integral feature of God's original plan for creation.

Another consideration of the Fall/Redemption Traditional Christian Story is to reflect on how the story is a symbolic expression of profound archetypal themes that are prevalent in ancient mythology. Myths of ancient mystery religions describe how the unity of creation (the Eden garden symbol) is shattered by primordial sin leading to suffering and mortality followed by restoration through redemption and resurrection. Unity with the gods is achieved through the birth-rebirth cycle of mystery religions. Does the Traditional Christian Story draw from the depths of ancient archetypal myths residing in the collective unconscious of humankind by naming Jesus as the Christ restoring humanity to divine reunification?

It needs to be emphasised again that the Traditional Christian Story is firmly grounded in the writings of the New Testament. Those who oppose any notion of an alternative orthodoxy insist that the Fall/Redemption Traditional Christian Story is the story that is most faithful to the New Testament. However, scripture scholars also remind us that the writers of the New Testament could only draw from their own Jewish traditions and religious affiliation to interpret the coming of Jesus as the Christ. God's revelation In Jesus as the Christ could only happen *within* a time-bound human consciousness and within the history and religious experiences of Israel. Any writings about Jesus as the Christ are always filtered through the human mind and consciousness of a particular era in the history and culture of first century Palestine. Theologies about the nature of revelation are undergoing a revision in the light of a better understanding of unitive consciousness. How God is revealed is always shaped by how revelation is interpreted through an historical lens.

Ken Wilber's discussion of the need in religions to 'transcend and include' is relevant here. Christianity needs to leave behind historical accretions that have complicated the integrity of the Jesus story. On the other hand, we do not leave behind past wisdoms which have been a rich source of religious practice and spirituality. A new story or alternative orthodoxy must transcend theological accretions of the Fall/Redemption story by including the basic beliefs and narratives of the Christian faith and propose a more coherent paradigm of the Christian experience in a new world of cosmic consciousness. Our contemporary consciousness is more global and ecumenical than those of previous ages.

While all the great world religions have been engaged in works for justice and promoting ethical standards, none of these religions have so far significantly recast their theologies and spiritualities within a cosmic and evolutionary framework (Delio 2015:98). The enterprise of composing an alternative orthodoxy is in its initial stages of articulation and has many steep hills of resistance from theological and official church systems to climb.

There is a growing readiness among contemporary Christians for a complementary Cosmic Christian Story which resonates with modern consciousness and scientific awareness. The complementary story will draw from traditions already within Christian spirituality and situate these wisdoms within an evolutionary cosmic consciousness. Such a complementary story will be more readily received by the faithful if the story is endorsed by the official teaching church as an alternative orthodoxy.

Currently, the alternative story is slowly emerging from a heightened awareness of the cosmic awareness of the Incarnation. Until the alternative orthodoxy is sanctioned by the official teaching church, the proponents of the Cosmic Christian Story will always have limited access to public opportunities for sharing the story and be subject to ecclesiastical scrutiny. I speak from personal experiences in ministry over many years and the interdicts against some of my theological peers.

Is it time to revise the paradigm of the Traditional Christian Story in the light of a dramatic shift in world consciousness shaped by the extraordinary developments in science?

> *What are your responses to the critique of the Traditional Christian Story?*
> *What aspects of the Traditional Christian Story do you find more difficult to accept or are you content to live your Christian faith as you presently experience it?*

Before we explore the complementary theology and spirituality of the Cosmic Christian Story, it would seem relevant and instructive at this juncture to divert from the theme of this chapter to examine an issue that is contentious for those resisting change: 'Does the church change its teaching?', 'Is it acceptable for the Christian community to celebrate a Cosmic Christian Story as an alternative orthodoxy to the Traditional Christian Story if the new story seems to offer an alternate lens to the official teachings of the church?'

Do Church teachings change?

The more conservative elements in the church insist that the teachings of the church never really change. However, such a position is simply untenable in the face of historical realities.

A *classical* consciousness insists that church teachings are timeless and never change.

An *historical* consciousness holds that church teachings are modified in the light of science, cultural shifts in consciousness and insights from historical studies.

There are numerous examples of the doctrinal changes in the 2000 year old evolution of the church's teachings. Scholars point out that for the first three hundred years of Christianity, there were many diverse theological positions held by the various churches especially in Antioch, Alexandria, Corinth and Rome. Only in more recent times have scholars uncovered Gnostic literature that influenced various schools of early Christian theology. The worldviews of those who lived in the medieval times are vastly different from the world views of those living today. Throughout the centuries, church teachings changed or were modified on such themes as God's revelation given to religious traditions other than Christianity, the role of the papacy, primacy of conscience, separation of church and state, slavery, usury (charging of interest on loans), inerrancy of the Bible, the veracity of evolution, religious freedom and so on. The documents composed during the Second Vatican Council (1962-1965) in the Catholic Church were a far cry from the *Syllabus of Errors* (1864) of Pius IX. The *Syllabus of Errors* was basically a denunciation of many features of modern civilisation that are now endorsed by the church and we take for granted.

In 1302 Pope Boniface VIII taught *extra ecclesiam, nulla salus* ('outside the church there is no salvation'). The Council of Florence (1438 -1445) defined this as a doctrine of the church to be held by all the faithful. The Second Vatican Council document 'Declaration on Religious Freedom' (1965) overturned that teaching. Notwithstanding the Second Vatican Council, the exclusive claim by the church to be only path to salvation is obviously deep in Catholic psyche. Even as recently as the year 2000, the teaching of Boniface VIII reappeared. In the Vatican Declaration *Dominus Jesus*, we read: 'Above all else it must be firmly believed that the Church, a pilgrim on earth, is necessary for salvation; the one Christ is the mediator and the way of salvation' (n 20). From the perspective of the five billion people who are not Christian, how such a document ever came to be composed in the year 2000 is almost beyond comprehension. This extraordinary claim for monopoly by the Christian Church for Christ as *the* path for salvation has now quietly dropped out of official church thinking.

To continue to hold that the teachings of the church never change is simply a denial of history. Other examples of changes in church teachings could readily be given.

In a conference to Italian church leaders (Florence October 2015), Pope Francis said, 'Church doctrine is not a closed system incapable of generating questions, doubts, interrogatives – but is alive, knows being unsettled, enlivened. It has a face that is not rigid, it has a body that moves and grows, it has soft flesh. It is called Jesus Christ'.

Fresh insights are garnered from the evolution of consciousness about humans in world and extraordinary advances in science, technology, cosmology and especially evolution. It is common sense to acknowledge that doctrines enunciated by scholars of past times need to be modified or even discarded when such doctrines are contradicted by proven scientific evidence and insights from the social sciences. For example, the designation of homosexual people as possessing 'a subjective disorder' is a case in point, reflecting cultural attitudes and a dysfunctional anthropology. Current ethical issues such as IVF, cloning, stem cell research, assisted dying, transgender, contraception, genetic modification, all ask questions about notions of moral absolutes and invite a Spirit nuanced discernment of ethical teachings.

Previous classical moral theology based on fixed abstract universal principles in natural law has given way to contemporary moral theology shaped by historical and life experience contexts. Some ideas and practices which were considered morally evil in one era (e.g. religious freedom) become a virtue in our world today. The shift in moral theology from fixed universal principles governed by natural law to an awareness of an historical and life experience context is illustrated in the growing movement to revise the teachings of *Humanae Vitae* (1968). The classical principle that all sexual intercourse must be open to procreation as a given dictum of natural law is now being orientated towards honouring the alternate principle of 'a deeply personal process for making decisions'. This principle was formulated by the Catholic Church's International Commission in 2009. With such threats as AIDS and the Zika virus to healthy birth, couples having sexual relations certainly need to engage in 'a deeply personal process for making decisions'. Furthermore moral theology still needs to be more grounded in the scriptures and more inclusive of global issues such as environmental concerns and inter-faith ethics.

The new science of emergence proposes that new properties come into existence out of elements in levels below but not including those elements. Emergence theory offers exciting possibilities for a Cosmic Christian narrative. How did water come from a mix of hydrogen and oxygen? The emergence model of science, when applied to the Christian story, alerts

Christians to a future prospect that the Christ narrative may assume different forms and practices while retaining the core elements of God's revelation in Jesus. Historical studies on the development of doctrine enlighten the Christian community in discarding those accumulations of teachings which obscure the Good News.

The central Christian doctrine of Incarnation insists that the Christ story is told and lived *within* the human condition not *outside* the web of life in the universe. For Christians, Jesus as the Christ is both a human and divine person who is of this world and not of this world. In the majestic opening words of the First Letter of John, we read, *We declare to you what was from the beginning, what we have heard, what we have seen with our eyes, what we have looked at and touched with our hands, concerning the word of life – this life was revealed* (1 John 1). Jesus is a source of life and he sought to make God more accessible and visible to people. Teachings about God's revelation in Christ will always be modified in the light of new wisdoms emanating from new consciousness. God's self-disclosure did not begin and end two thousand years ago but is always evolving in human consciousness. Revelation is always a developing and expanding process of illuminating the divine mysteries. Christianity may well be flourishing among future human civilisations on the planet Mars in the year 3000 and God's self-communication will assume very different forms than its present expressions on earth.

The Christian Story must embrace the evolutionary story of the universe if the Incarnation is to honour the oneness of the human/divine revelation of God in Jesus. Our biological origins emanate from massive explosions of supernovas. Thus any reflection on the humanity of Jesus evokes questions about our own biological origins and the nature of our own humanity in the cosmos.

Modern science raises disturbing questions about the traditional understanding of the status of humans within the web of life in the universe. The Copernicus revolution displaced a previous human understanding of us as the centre of the universe. From a position of pre-eminence on earth, astrophysics after Copernicus and Galileo seemed to say that we are but tiny specks of isolated beings in a vast and impersonal universe. Darwin's description of the evolution of humans from primitive material further reinforced a perceived relativity of the human species, descended as we are from stardust. Reinforcing the prospect of cosmic loneliness for humankind in the limitless spaces of the universe, cosmology demonstrated that the earth is a small planet among billions of planets within billions of galaxies. Sometimes when gazing at the winking stars in the night sky, we can be overwhelmed by its beauty and arches of diffused light. During other times, while scanning the Milky Way, we may experience feelings of how insignificant we really are as alien spectators in the cosmos with its billions of galaxies.

Modern theology has only just taken a few tentative steps to retell the Christ story within a cosmic context and absolutely disputes any suggestion of humanity's insignificance in the universe. In a Christian vision of life, each person is precious in God's eyes, *For God so loved the world that he gave his only Son, so that everyone who believes in him but may have eternal life* (John 3:16). The Cosmic Christian Story makes sense now that we are more aware of our critical role within our wondrous universe, especially as humans are the most significant influence on the wellbeing or otherwise of a healthy biosphere. We observe and experience climate changes that are impacting on food resources, world health, migration and increasing levels of species extinction. Evolution is a *becoming* happening. Do we choose to be positive agents in embracing the possibilities for humanity and creation or do we stand aside and allow the opportunity to pass us by? For Christians, a key question is whether Christ is within this evolutionary vision or whether Christ is understood as outside a cosmic vision and focused solely on personal salvation.

To retreat from this enterprise of reshaping the Cosmic Christian Story out of fear of marginalisation or exclusion by the official church will gradually consign the Christian narrative to an historical oddity. The magnificent Christian story is too precious and relevant for all humanity to be lost in a forest of theological disputation, intellectual timidity and non-discerning exercise of ecclesiastical authority. Our era is at a turning point for the Christian story if God's revelation in Jesus is to be firmly embedded into a cosmic vision of the universe. Religious authorities are to be encouraged to promote informed conversations and openness to a discernment of the Spirit.

Tradition is not some static object chained to a post of past times.

Tradition is a living energising story which is being told and retold in the light of past memories and new life-Spirit experiences.

Each higher level of consciousness invites Christians to *Stay awake* (Matthew 26:41) lest they miss Christ passing by in their world about them.

> *In your own faith journey, share your views about changes in the church teachings. Which changes have most affected on how you live your Christian faith?*
>
> *What further information would you like to know about how doctrines develop in the story of the church through the ages?*

Conclusion

Our epoch is calling Christians to explore a more fruitful appreciation of our relationships with God in Christ within the wonder of an evolving universe.

The following chapters will consider the theology and spirituality of the alternative orthodoxy, beginning with the majestic story of God's creation of the universe.

The theology and spirituality of this narrative have some different perspectives from the Traditional Christian Story and a different impulse for the Incarnation

What do we understand by the Cosmic Christian Story?

CHAPTER FOUR

Features of a Cosmic Christian Story: the beginnings

> *While such stories will no doubt be told far into the future, a new integrating story has emerged. Even though it is only a few centuries old, it has already begun to change humanity in crucial ways. This is the story of the universe's development through time, the narrative of the evolutionary processes of our observable universe. The story has, and will continue to have, many different names. But if we can think of the New Testament as that which tells a Christian story, and of the 'Mahabharata' as that which tells a Hindu story, perhaps the simplest description of this new narrative is that it tells a universe story.*
>
> Brian Thomas Swimme & Mary Evelyn Tucker,
> *Journey of the Universe.* 3

This age of consciousness has created a cultural readiness to tell the unfolding Christian story within a new cosmic framework. The traditional framework with its assumptions about the three-tiered world and fallen humanity in the Traditional Christian Story has to be enlarged or modified to embrace a vision of the new cosmology and modern science. Scientific truth and religious truth are not irreconcilable nor is scientific truth more valid than religious truth or vice versa. Both scientific truth and religious truth aspire to greater insight and wisdom into the mysteries of the universe and our place within the web of life.

Modern science is a driving force that is reshaping how we see the world and fostering a new consciousness. Quantum physics shows how everything in the universe is connected and dynamic in its emergence. Everything that we see which may seem solid to us is actually made up of tiny particles which can be converted into enormous energy.

A startling feature of quantum physics is that nothing is real unless it is observed and that uncertainty is a principle within nature itself. Various theorists, such as the physicist Neils Bohr (1885 – 1962) and associates, claim that something can have a wave or particle nature depending on the perspective of the observer. Ilia Delio sums up a scientific position about quantum physics by her statement, *It is meaningless to ascribe any properties or even existence to anything that has not been measured.* What quantum physics tells us is that *nothing is real unless it is observed* (2015: 43). The subjectivity of quantum physics, in contrast to the certainty of Newtonian physics, generates caution in scientists about making absolute predictions, instead of probabilities. The theologian Diarmuid O'Murchu questions the validity of any assumptions which suggest 'that, we humans, at this stage in our evolution, can pronounce the final word on how things are in the universe' (1997:104). Nature has its own laws which science is slowly discovering (cf Edwards 2010, 84-85). It seems rather arrogant for humans to imagine that they have the ultimate wisdom to know and determine the laws of nature. Who knows what the future holds for humans in the evolutionary story of the universe? Perhaps *Homo sapiens* in the future may be surpassed by higher forms of developed creatures who possess superior capacities to thrive on earth and other planets. If this scenario eventuates what will be the response to the question, *Who do you say I am?*

The scientific search for knowledge to unlock the mysteries of the universe raises very complex questions of epistemology (how we know). When we seek to uncover the mysteries of the universe, is our knowing always valid for everyone? The famous *cogito ergo sum* ('I think therefore I am') of Rene Descartes (1596 – 1650) separated a person from the external world. According to Descartes any reality is only what I perceive to be reality. If we agree with Descartes' *cogito*, then the world we know is only our mind's understanding of the world. Such an epistemology renders humanity as planetary orphans, divorced from participating in the mysteries of the external world. Immanuel Kant tried to soften the human centrism of Descartes by describing how knowledge is related to experience but knowledge is not confined to one's experience of the world. The wonders of nature are not waiting around for humans to discover their beauty and diversity. The uncertainty principle embedded in quantum physics reinforced a caution about absolute laws in knowing. Notwithstanding this indecision in fixed laws about science, contemporary science has bypassed an epistemological paralysis and forged ahead in utilising scientific advances to construct a modern world. Not always have these advances been conducive to the earth's wellbeing. Given the probability, not certainty in quantum physics, the epistemological question remains, 'How do we come to know about our being and knowing in the universe?' For Christians, the Cosmic Christian Story offers a faith vision of being and knowing within this universe.

Although science has advanced our knowledge of the universe exponentially, we recognise that we have hardly scratched the surface of scientific knowledge about the universe. Ninety-five per cent of non-matter in the universe is 69% dark energy and 26% dark matter. What dark energy actually is baffles scientists. The discovery of the merging of two black holes in creating gravitational waves in 2016 proved that black holes do exist. Recently, a black hole with a mass of 17 billion suns has been discovered in a large isolated galaxy 200 million light years away. A new analysis by the University of Indiana estimates that there are at least a trillion species on the planet and 99.9% have not yet been fully identified. In 2016, NASA announced that the Kepler Space Telescope Mission had discovered the largest collection of planets (1,200) ever sighted.

When we reflect of the magnificent hymn of God's creation described in Genesis Chapter 1, we are puzzled how this primal cosmic vision was largely marginalised in the development of Christian theology. Over the centuries, Christianity theology became more and more focused on the personal sinfulness of the human condition. During the first few centuries, Christian theology rapidly became impregnated with Gnosticism and neo-platonic dualism. A body/spirit split began to shape Christian spirituality and contradict the essential oneness of the Incarnation. The anthropocentric paradigm became the basic framework for theologising about God and the mission of Christ. For the credibility of future Christianity, the anthropocentric (the person as the centre) focus on humanity alone has to be revised and supplanted by a cosmocentric (the cosmos as the centre) vision of all things in the universe. The dysfunctional anthropology of the Fall/Redemption paradigm should now be replaced by a positive anthropology that celebrates the human species as an integral element within the web of all life in an evolutionary universe.

The divine energy of creation was fully involved in the evolution of the universe for billions of years, long before humankind emerged. It would be bizarre for anyone to envisage that the real story of creation began with the advent of humans. Such a worldview would suggest that somehow the previous 13.7 billion years were a mere backdrop patiently waiting for some form of hominids to appear three million years ago and *Homo sapiens* to finally take centre stage of the universe during the last 150,000 years. A Cosmic Christian Story embraces the whole span of creation, beginning 13.7 years ago. God's primal revelation happened with the initial act of creation.

The following description of the Cosmic Christian Story explains the main evolutionary themes as a framework for a contemporary understanding of the Christ experience within creation.

The evolutionary story

A massive outburst of explosive energy (Big Bang) happens in 13.7 billion years ago and within a million years the first atoms of hydrogen begin to undergo fusion to form other elements such as helium and lithium.

Everything that we have or will have in the universe, everything that we are or will be, every single element in the universe, all were contained is that primal massive fireball 13.7 billion years ago.

About 12 billion years ago, the first stars and galaxies form. The early stars were intensely hot, exploding as giant supernovas sending out elements which gradually condensed into new stars. As a result of nuclear reactions taking place in these stars, our Milky Way begins to form about 8 billion years ago.

Our solar system forms about 4.7 billion years ago.

The first cells of life as algae and bacteria emerge 3.5 billion years ago. At first there were single cells then multi-cellular organisms such as trilobites, shells, fish, amphibians, reptiles, grass, insects, flowers, birds and mammals.

About 542 million years ago, there is an extraordinary outburst of life in the Cambrian period followed by the Great Dying (488 million years ago) where 80 - 90% of all life became extinct.

The Devonian period (395 million years ago) is followed by the Carboniferous period (350 million years ago) and the Permian period (256 million years ago). During the Permian period, the third Great Dying happens (245 million years ago) with 75-90% of all species becoming extinct.

The Triassic extinction (200 million years ago) was followed by the dominant dinosaur era which lasted for 150 million years. During the Jurassic (150million years ago) and Cretaceous (125 million years ago) periods, a variety of life becomes much more abundant and diverse.

(cf Swimme B. T. & Tucker M. E. *Journey of the Universe*, 119 - 131)

Share your understanding of the evolution of the universe and what does this evolution say to your Christian faith?

The advent of humanity

In the story of the universe, humans are very late arrivals on the scene. In the well-known cosmic calendar of the cosmologist Carl Sagan and the conferences of the astrophysicist Neil deGrasse Tyson, the story of the universe is described as a year beginning January 1st. According to the cosmic calendar, humans finally appeared a few minutes before midnight December 31st.

During the Pliocene (5 million years ago) and Pleistocene (1.5 million years ago) periods, a wide variety of animals emerge as well as the first humans (*Homo habilis* and *Homo erectus*).

Humans possess a common genetic ancestry with all living things on the earth. Every single atom in our body has originated from monstrous supernova explosions billions of years ago. DNA is the genetic code common to all life. Humans share a 99.9% identical DNA with apes and also share a DNA connection with other elements in the plant and sea life. Various branches of the *hominid* species came into being. There was no direct line from these species to modern people. Rather there was a very diverse mix of *hominid* in the evolutionary story of the human race with self-survival the determining factor if a strand of *hominid* would survive.

About 150,000 years ago, the first strand of modern human species (*Homo sapiens*) emerges and begins the great journey across the globe emanating 'out of Africa'. The other human strands gradually disappear. It is estimated that the Neanderthal strand of *hominid* died out about 23,000 years ago. Recently, a third major strand of *hominid* has been discovered. The Denisovan DNA indicates that this strand roamed far and wide across Siberia and into South-East Asia. *Homo sapiens* emerged as the only surviving form of the human species. The species *Homo sapiens* was characterised by enlarged brains that enabled this species to experience self-consciousness, symbolic and linguistic capacities and freedom to make choices. In a certain sense, *Homo sapiens* became the *consciousness* of all life forms on the earth. In the Genesis sacred myth, at some evolutionary stage *Homo sapiens* was formed in 'the image and likeness of God' (Genesis 1:27). For people of religious faith, at what stage did the *hominid* species cross a consciousness threshold to be created 'in the image and likeness of God'? This core question is a matter of theological speculation and cannot be verified by science.

Humans settling the earth

From about 10,000 years ago, humans began to settle in small villages and towns especially along the banks of the great rivers such as the Euphrates, the Nile, Ganges and the Yellow river. The cultivation of wheat, barley, squash, beans, maize, rice, potatoes and quinoa enabled gatherings of people to be fed and develop the first urban dwellings.

By about 3,000 BCE, the population of *Homo sapiens* had grown to perhaps 5 -8 million. The first forms of settled civilisation appear along the Nile valley in Egypt and cuneiform writing in Sumer begins to replace the monopoly of oral traditions in cultures. During the Axial period (800 BCE-300 BCE), philosophical thinking from the Greeks (Socrates, Plato, Aristotle), Confucius in China, Buddha and the Four Noble Truths in India, all raised human consciousness to another level of personal and spiritual awareness.

Emergence of religion

Anthropologists have uncovered widespread evidence of human beliefs about divine spirits and desires to relate to the spirit world. Early humans accepted that they were intimately connected to the whole intricate patterns of life in the universe. Their very survival depended on their relationships in placating these spirits and acknowledging their presence. They lived on the edge of existence where a famine or flood could wipe out their means of survival. The spirits of nature must be brought into some kind of friendly relationship. For thousands of years, humans lived a spiritual existence keenly aware of the mystery of life around them. Many indigenous tribes held some form of animism and worshipped fertility goddesses such as the Great Mother. Some burial sites of ancient people showed evidence of food left for the afterlife. Indigenous tribes, such as Australian Aborigines, related to the earth as their Mother who provided them with sustenance and spiritual meaning. The Australian Aborigines told stories of the Dreamtime. In South Sea Islands, the spirit force was *mana*. In Arabian culture, the numinous force was *jinn*.

It is important to distinguish between religion and spirituality. About 5000 years ago, history describes the gradual emergence of formal religions. The word 'religion' comes from the Latin *re- ligio* meaning 'to bring together', 'to reunite'. The 'bringing together' is a reuniting of self, community, divinity and creation in more formal structures and communal worship.

As towns, city-states and empires developed, local deities and cults became marginalised or even suppressed. People increasingly began to worship in more central and organised forms of religion. During the Axial Age humanity experienced a pivotal leap in spiritual maturation. During the Axial Age, we see the emergence of the great faiths that have profoundly influenced humanity ever since that time. Buddhism and Hinduism in India, Confucianism and Taoism in China, the monotheism of Judaism in the Middle East, the philosophies and rationalism in Greece, all were manifestations of this new genre of spirituality and source of relating to the numinous in people's experience.

There are now signs that a Second Axial Age is emerging, beginning perhaps in the early 20th century. This Second Axial Age heralds a new phase in religious consciousness. The first Axial Age highlighted individual consciousness. The Second Axial Age is more orientated towards a global, inclusive communal consciousness.

Salient features of this emerging Second Axial Age include the following:

- Global in scope
- Recognition of a pluralism of truths in various religions
- Relational spirituality
- Committed to peace and justice
- Integrating the diverse aspects of knowing
- Emphasising wisdom as the key to holistic learning in a digital age
- Supporting human rights
- Oneness with the earth community
- Spirituality for all
- De-emphasis on the system dimensions of religions.

The emerging Second Axial Age confronts Christianity with formidable challenges and also exciting opportunities for a transformation of its mission in sharing the Good News.

What does the story of the evolution of religions say to the story of Christianity?

The birth of Christianity

The Christian story was born within the womb of Judaism. The first followers of Jesus were Jews and believed that they were in continuity with the story of God's chosen people of Israel. Jewish texts prophesied that a Messiah would come and set the people of Israel free from oppression. Only after the death and resurrection of Jesus as the Christ did Christian orthodoxy slowly evolve during the first three centuries.

Jesus grew up in the remote village of Nazareth in the northern region of Galilee. He felt called to preach his message of the reign of God. Jesus went about the countryside healing and teaching. His country background is reflected in his down-to-earth images and parables about the reign of God: farmers sowing seeds, lost sheep, lilies in the field, dishonest landlords, wheat, fig trees and wayward children. The proclamation of the reign of God was a clarion call for a new time of justice, healing and experiencing a God of love and care, especially for the dispossessed. His teachings were fully in accord with Jewish beliefs and teachings, especially with the prophetic voices in Israel. After about three years of his public teachings, Jesus was deemed a threat to the religious and political establishment. He was captured and crucified by the Roman authorities. Jesus died an excruciating death as an sacrificial act of solidarity with all those who suffer for just causes and attuned to the universal 'groaning of creation' (Romans 8:23).

According to early Christian beliefs, Jesus was raised up by God in resurrection as the Christ. After his death and resurrection, the disciples of Jesus, filled with joy, preached about God's revelation in Jesus as the Christ. At Pentecost, the Spirit empowered and emboldened these disciples to courageously tell people about the Good News of the gospel. The Christian faith community was born at Pentecost. Within a very short time, early Christian communities spread rapidly across the world. It took almost three hundred years before orthodox Christology affirmed that Jesus as the Christ was fully God and man, the divine Word of God. Today, there are about two billion Christians in every country.

In theological circles, there is much debate about the transformation of the Jesus experience of his mission to the Christology in the writings of Paul. The topic is too complex for elaboration in this book and has been mentioned previously in Chapter Two. Suffice to say here that the Christology of Paul laid the foundations of the Fall/Redemption Story by insisting that it was only through Christ that humans found access to God (cf Romans 5:1, 5:9). There have been at least SEVEN major phases in the 2000 year old Christian story:

1. Birth of the Christian movement
2. Spread of Christianity during the Roman Empire and beyond the Empire
3. The epoch of Christendom in Europe
4. Reformation and the global spread of Christianity, including Asia, Africa, Americas
5. The challenge of the Enlightenment in Western countries
6. Christianity in a post-modern world and evangelisation
7. Globalisation and Christianity.

Another epoch in the story of Christianity is now unfolding. This period is shaped by a raised consciousness emerging out of scientific worldviews, especially an evolutionary appreciation of the universe. This developing phase in the Christian story is moving Christianity to a higher plane of global consciousness that is fashioning an alternative orthodoxy for Christian believers.

A defining feature of this growing consciousness is what is called 'relationality'.

Relationality explains that everything that exists in the human, animal, natural and cosmic world is in relationships with one another. Scientific theories during the last hundred years have consistently espoused the connectedness of all things in the universe. The science of relationality strongly resonates with religious beliefs about the divine oneness of all things in creation and a universal energy of love. Relationality rejects the fragmentation of society, tribalism, economic cultism and selfish individualism.

In our time of the Christian story, there is a growing movement to return to the core vision of God's revelation in Jesus through the Spirit. Biblical studies, history and archaeology have illuminated the Jesus story within the cultural milieu of first century Palestine. The proclamation, *And the Word became flesh and lived among us* (John 1:14) invites all Christians to ground the meaning of the Incarnation firmly within an evolutionary cosmos. Historical studies on the development of Christian doctrine illuminate how some accumulated doctrines have distorted or even contradicted the primal revelation of God in Jesus. As explained earlier in Chapter Three, the doctrines of original sin, literalism of atonement and 'outside the church there is no salvation' are examples of doctrines which diminished the teachings of Jesus.

The contemporary world envisages a much broader vision of religion. It is proposed in this book that the development of an alternative orthodoxy for Christians is helpful if Christianity is to be more aligned with this higher level of consciousness. The paradox of this movement towards an emerging level of consciousness for a global spirituality is a contrary growth of fundamentalism (cf Armstrong 2000). As discussed earlier, how in times of rapid cultural change groups sometimes revert to previous securities as a response to coping with uncertainty. Fear of the unknown becomes the driving energy of fundamentalism.

An initial impulse for this quest for an alternative Christian orthodoxy is to address Christians with two core questions:

What was (is) the mission of Jesus?

Why did the Incarnation happen?

The Fall/Redemption tradition taught that Jesus came to repair the breakdown of relationship with God through the sin of our First Parents. His mission was interpreted as one of redemption for the sins of humankind and reveal God as a loving Presence.

In the light of modern science and cosmology, there are some issues of how this Fall-Redemption paradigm is in accord recent biblical studies. Some of these problems have already been discussed in Chapter Three.

What is your viewpoint about why the Incarnation happened, in other words, why did Jesus come into the world?

How do we read the Bible?

Once again, we need divert from the main thread of this chapter to address a question which underpins much of the discussion about a critique of the Traditional Christian Story. The topic has been considered earlier but until Christians learn to read the Bible with a basic appreciation of hermeneutics, then the spiritual wisdoms of the scriptures will always be obscured by literalism and cherry picking of selected texts. If it seems repetitive in returning to the problem of literalism, my experiences of many years in pastoral ministry have reinforced the reality of how the majority of Christians are still steeped in biblical literalism and doctrinal fundamentalism. Even recently, during a homily, the congregation were reminded that as Catholics, when they went to Communion they are required to believe that they are eating the flesh of Christ! Literalism is a major element in the theological framework of the Traditional Christian Story (see Tacey).

Related to any critique of the Fall/Redemption Story is the question of how people use and understand the Bible.

How we read the bible is a critical concern in people's image of God. An ignorance of basic principles of hermeneutics traps one into the tyranny of literalism. A biblical image of God is almost invariably male reinforcing the patriarchal power structures of Judaism and Christianity. Some of the biblical images of God which we read in the Hebrew scripture evoke revulsion and disbelief in such a deity. We read about a vengeful God who caused the earth to be flooded in the Noah story (Genesis 6); a deity who punishes sinners by plagues (Exodus 8 - 11); a god who caused the sun to stand still so the extermination of enemies could continue until they were all slain (Joshua 10:13); a god who kills off all first born children in Egypt enabling the Israelites to escape (Exodus 12). During Holy Thursday liturgy I always cringe when the final verses of the Exodus reading of the Passover story is proclaimed, *For I will pass through the land of Egypt that night, and I will strike down every first born in the land of Egypt, both human beings and animals; on all the gods of Egypt I will execute judgments: I am the Lord* (Exodus 12:12).

Modern science, not God, demonstrates how climate changes, how tsunamis form, how shifting tectonic plates cause earthquakes and how evolution unfolds in its complexity. In evolutionary history, there have been five major extinctions of species, beginning towards the end of the Cambrian period 480 million years ago. The birth and death cycle is a regular feature of changing evolutionary patterns. As discussed earlier in the book, a literalist reading of the Bible and ignorance of the process of how doctrines evolve, inhibit an openness to discern how the Spirit is speaking to Christians through communal consciousness moving to a higher level.

Share some of the challenges you face when you read the Bible.

A complementary explanation for the advent and mission of the Christ experience is one that is set firmly within the evolutionary story of the universe.

> *How does the great story of the universe and humans impact on your religious beliefs?*
> *Why might some people have problems with reconciling evolution and their religious faith?*

Conclusion

This chapter has described a scientific account of the evolution of the universe and the advent of humans. The Cosmic Christian Story is situated within this great story. To better appreciate the Cosmic Christian Story, Christians need to be more conversant with the principles of hermeneutics in their reading and meditation on the Bible.

The following chapter develops the theme of a cosmocentric explanation of the Incarnation.

Chapter Five

Understanding the Cosmic Christian Story

Our insistence that each human being is an image of God should not make us overlook the fact that each creature has its own purpose. None is superfluous. The entire material universe speaks of God's love, his boundless affection for us. Soil, water, mountains: everything is, as it were, a caress of God.

Pope Francis: Laudato si, n 84.

We may be seeing the beginning of the reintegration of our culture, a new possibility of the unity of consciousness. If so, it will not be on the basis of any new orthodoxy, either religious or scientific. Such a new integration will be based on the rejection of all univocal understandings of reality, of all identifications of one conception of reality with reality itself. It will recognise the multiplicity of the human spirit, and the necessity to translate constantly between different scientific and imaginative vocabularies.

Robert Bellah Beyond Belief

The movement towards articulating the Christian Cosmic Story has been stimulated by the paradigm shift in a scientific understanding of the nature of being itself and our place in the cosmic order. If the Incarnation means anything, Incarnation happens within this mysterious world of relationships that enfolds us. By trying to better understand, even at a basic level, the new and changing scientific view of the world, we deepen our appreciation of Jesus who, as divine and human, entered this world and resurrected as the Christ. God created the world to bring all things into a divine unity of relationships. Almost 1000 years ago, Thomas Aquinas (d 1274) warned us about the urgency of seeking right relationships between God and creation. His views may be summarised by: 'If we get creation wrong, we get God wrong' (see Tarnas 180 – 181).

Let us revisit some relevant trends in modern science that have already been discussed but are helpful in understanding how these scientific advances resonate with key features of a Cosmic Christian Story.

The dawning of a new cosmology might be marked in the 16th century when the astronomer Nicolaus Copernicus offered a new vision of the cosmos and humanity's place in it. Copernicus proposed that the sun, not the earth, was the centre of the universe. Almost a hundred years later in 1610, Galileo Galilei supported Copernicus' theory that planet earth is circling the sun. The British scientist Isaac Newton in his major work *The Principia* (1687) described laws that governed gravity. In 1859, Charles Darwin published his momentous work *The origin of Species by Natural Selection*, opening the way for an understanding of how evolution happens. In Darwin's explanation of evolution, there were gradual modifications of life forms over time and then new species emerged through a process of natural selection. An Austrian monk Gregor Mendel (1822-1884), through his experiments with pea plants, set out the principles of heredity and laid the foundations of modern genetics. During the twentieth century, quantum physics eroded any mechanistic views about the universe by highlighting a relational world of energy fields.

A basic feature of a modern scientific view of the world is the interrelatedness of all things. According to the theologian Ilia Delio, 'Relationship is not a *quality* of being, as Aristotle taught, it *is* being' (2011: 27). Early in the 20th century, quantum physics overturned the predictable theories about movements of bodies within a system. Matter is not made up as a series of building blocks but rather a web of relations. The very nature of everything in the world is one of relationships or relationality. The term 'relationality' has been explained earlier in Chapter Four.

The physicist David Bohm's theory of 'implicate order' stated that the state of being is not only relational but exists as an unbroken wholeness in a system. There is an essential oneness which links all things, including all people, at the deepest level. The scientist James Lovelock (b 1919) proposed the Gaia hypothesis which stated that the earth is one organic whole body in which everything is interrelated.

Modern physics proposes that humans exist in a whole variety of energy fields that shape the ways we are and how we act. Humans live in a kind of huge ocean of energy which swirls and washes everywhere, connecting every single thing in the universe, including humans. The British biologist Rupert Sheldrake (b 1942) described how people are linked through 'morphogenetic' fields which carry knowledge and behaviour through a process called 'morphic resonance'. The theory of morphic resonance explains how an individual organism can be influenced by the behaviour of another organism of the same species (MacGregor 64-69). Prayers for others move across these energy fields to influence those people. Sheldrake's theory offers a possible understanding of how influential people, such as Francis of Assisi or the Buddha, can affect the lives of people on a global scale and across space and time. We all have experienced at some time the positive energy that has touched us from inspirational people. Every time I hear Martin Luther King Jr.'s 'I have a dream' speech I am moved almost to tears. A Christian belief holds that the Universal or Cosmic Christ is an expression of a force energy field moving beyond time/space and national borders. Through morphic resonance, Christ affects the whole of humanity with the Christ energy of universal love. The death of Jesus on the cross is a sacrificial redemptive act that moves in energy fields as a healing power for brokenness and sinfulness in the world.

Within fields of energy there is a self-organising principle which impels and shapes evolutionary changes. Scientists call this universal organising principle 'consciousness' or 'mind'. The 'mind' seems to be some kind of impulse which allows entities to form and cooperate with other entities. It is consciousness which seems to be the power that holds all things in the universe together. In a religious framework, it is the divine consciousness which is creator, sustainer and energiser of everything in the universe. In Colossians, we read, *all things have been created through him and for him. He himself is before all things, and in him all things hold together* (1:16 -17).

According to the Ilya Prigogine's theory of emergence, new systems are created in an evolutionary process out of sub-systems. However, elements in the new systems do not necessarily reside in the sub-systems. New entities are created almost mysteriously in an evolutionary upwards movement of greater complexity. The spontaneous appearances of new forms of life have different elements from previous elements. Emergence theory illustrates how nature itself amazingly possesses wonderful powers to generate new forms of matter. Nature has its own ways of being fertile in giving birth to unprecedented matter. From a faith perspective, the theologian Elizabeth Johnson has an interesting comment on the phenomena of emergence. She writes, 'Pondering this reality, Karl Rahner proposes that we embrace a fundamental idea: matter has the capacity to transcend itself. Matter can do this because it has been endowed by its Creator with an inner tendency, a quiet, powerfully pulsing drive, to become more' (2014: 175). What might be a 'more' response to the question, *Who do you say I am?*

The science of emergence is a possible model for the evolution of an alternative orthodoxy. Who is the Christ in an alternative orthodoxy? The Word, as the energy of God as creator, entered the world as human flesh and participates in the evolutionary story of creation itself, *In the beginning was the Word, and the Word was with God, and the Word was God... And the Word became flesh and lived among us* (John 1: 1, 14).

The oneness of all things in God began with the Big Bang. The 'cosmic Incarnation' (Richard Rohr) happened when 'the wind of God (*ruah*) swept over the face of the waters' (Genesis 1:2). The Greek word 'theos' meaning 'God' is derived from the Greek verb 'theo' meaning 'flow' or 'run' (Newell: 12). God is the ONE who flows or runs through all things. As Newell explains, creation emerges from the 'flow of God'. The whole of the universe is alive with the dynamism of the energising Spirit of creation. The fecundity of the Divine breath or *nephesh* generates all life. The birthing of the energy of the creator generates the Word into Jesus as the Christ. The central message of Jesus in his ministry was to continue and enhance the activity of the Divine breath to bring life to all (John 10:10).

There is no radical distinction between matter and Spirit. The concept of dualism which viewed a separation of matter and spirit is alien to the oneness of creation. If Christians explain Christ as the manifestation of God's energy in creation, then the eternal Christ is in creation from the beginning, that is, a 'cosmic Incarnation'. In Colossians we read, *He is the image of the invisible God, the first born of all creation; for in him all things in heaven and on earth were created, things visible and invisible, whether thrones or dominations or ruler or powers - all things have been created through him and for him* (Colossians 1:15 -16).

What are some scientific developments that hold real promise for an alternative orthodoxy of the Christian faith? Which scientific developments seem to pose a threat to the Christian narrative?

Deification or theosis is the core of the mission of Jesus

The starting point for the Cosmic Christian Story is not a failure in God's original plan for creation because of the purported sin of Adam and Eve but the wondrous beginning of creation itself with an explosion of creative energy.

Humans evolved over millions of years from more primitive forms of life. By their very nature, humans possessed the power to make choices for good or evil and to accumulate knowledge. The emergence of human consciousness empowered humans to know something of the divine within their being and the matrix of life around them.

In Genesis we read,

So God created humankind in his image, in the image of God he created them; male and female he created them (1:27).

Most major religions aspire to help people form a relationship with the Divine by fostering spirituality. The quest for union with God or gods is the ultimate goal of most religions. Buddhism teaches about this aspiration from a different path through enlightenment of the human condition of suffering. For the Buddha, how we live our present life is the important concern. In the Hindu scriptures of *Bhagavad Gita*, the god Krishna explains that all our actions should be dedicated to God and we must not seek to earn salvation by merit but by an unselfish commitment to the divine. Muslims experience union with Allah through fidelity to the Five Pillars of Islam. The mystical tradition of *kabbalah* in Judaism is a process of learning access to the Jewish wisdoms of spirituality. The ultimate purpose of Sikhism is to enter a state of mystical union with God.

The concept of 'salvation' is not concerned exclusively with something that happens after death. Salvation is an orientation towards the inner quest to become more god-like. The Greek origin of the word 'salvation' is *sozo* meaning 'to restore' or 'to make whole'. Such a spiritual understanding of salvation affirms the belief that becoming 'more whole' is becoming more god-like. Salvation is an ongoing process of how we live holistically by allowing the ebbs and flows of our lives to be touched by grace.

How does one become more god-like?

How is the 'image and likeness of God' interiorised in each person?

In a Cosmic Christian Story, this life journey for deepening the 'image and likeness of God' becomes the focused energy of God's presence within creation.

Jesus who became the Christ was born into creation to witness to oneness with God by the union of his being as God/Man. His life and teachings highlight how this quest for nurturing the 'image and likeness of God' may be better realised in everyday life.

In the evolution of consciousness over millions of years, Christians believe that cultural levels of consciousness 2000 years ago were at levels of readiness for Jesus to appear, born of his parents Mary and Joseph. God's revelation to Israel in the Hebrew Scriptures gradually illuminated a God of mercy and intimacy.

In his teachings, healing and life style, Jesus taught a way of holiness. The core of his teaching was the fostering of life, *I came that they may have life and have it abundantly* (John 10:10). In the prophetic tradition of Israel, Jesus announced the reign of God and the need for a conversion to a new life within God's love and grace. To nurture the divine image within oneself, Jesus proclaimed that one must seek to enhance life, life within oneself, others, creation and, above all, experience intimacy with God. Jesus encouraged his followers to seek this divine union by sharing his own union with God, *Do you not believe that I am in the Father and the Father is in me* (John 14:10); *On that day you will know that I am in the Father, and you are in me, and I in you* (John 14:20).

The mission of Jesus was not a restoration of a divine plan that went wrong with the purported sin of Adam and Eve, but a positive movement to help all people participate in the divine life of God through the Spirit (2 Peter:1:4). There is no such a thing as inherited sin but rather sin as personal choices that distort the image and likeness of God within us. Sin is being estranged from the impulse of realising more fully the 'image and likeness of God' within oneself and world. The preaching of Jesus about the reign of God and the injunction to live its values are intended to show how the 'image and likeness of God' might be experienced. The life, teachings, sacrificial death and resurrection of Jesus are the prototype of the human experience of a redemptive journey towards wholeness in God. Redemption is the process of liberating the person from addictions that impede the realisation of being created in 'the image and likeness of God'.

Everything in creation has its cycle of birth, death and transformation. We know in our own lives how setbacks and sufferings can lead us to personal growth. Who has not experienced loneliness, pain, sickness and alienation? How do we learn compassion without enduring suffering ourselves? Within the vision of the Cosmic Christian Story, the cross of the crucified Jesus is a symbol of the cosmic cross of birth, death and regeneration of all things in creation. The price of evolutionary growth of all things is high. In the evolutionary story of the universe, most species have perished, especially in the five 'Great Dyings'. Without the extinction of dinosaurs about 65 million years ago, many versions of mammals could never have emerged into life on the planet. If the giant meteor which crashed into the earth and set up a radical climate change that killed the dinosaurs had been a fraction earlier or later to miss the earth, would the hominid species have appeared? Life on earth lives and dies on a knife edge in the cycle of existence. Paul writes about the trauma of all things in creation, *We know that the whole creation has been groaning in labour pains until now; and not only the creation, but we ourselves, who have the first fruits of the Spirit, groan inwardly while we wait for adoption, the redemption of our bodies* (Romans 8:22-23).

The redemptive mission of Christ is freeing humanity to become more positively involved in the evolutionary process of creation. Humanity was never out of favour with God. Redemption is allowing the energies of humanity to be more attuned to God, the Source of love. According to the scripture scholar Marcus J. Borg (93), there are at least five interpretations of the suffering and death of Jesus, one of which is the symbolic act of dying to the old life of the law and being raised up to a new life of the Spirit, moving beyond the Outer Exterior Self to the True Inner Self of being, *For through the Law I died to the Law, so that I might live to God. I have been crucified with Christ; and it is no longer I who live, but it is Christ who lives in me* (Galatians 3:19 -20).

The cross is an evocative symbol of the price to be paid for fidelity to the mission of liberation. Calvary speaks to us about solidarity with all suffering endured during the underside of life. Jesus bravely faced the consequences of his radical message for justice which threatened the power structures of his society. This sacrificial act of Jesus on the cross is carried through energy fields as redemptive healing. In John's gospel, we read *Instead, one of the soldiers pierced his side with a spear, and at once blood and water came out* (19: 34). The spear of suffering releases a restorative flow of love and new life. The fidelity of Jesus to his mission of liberation illuminates God's willingness to express a love that is beyond reason. For a Christian, the Christ is the manifestation of God's presence in infusing all creation with the energy of the Spirit towards wholeness, *He himself is before all things, and in him all things hold together* (Colossians 1:17).

Deification or Theosis

This quest for deification or theosis is a core doctrine in Orthodox Byzantine theology and a highly relevant spirituality for all people today.

A theology and spirituality of deification are foundational features of the Cosmic Christian Story.

Who do you say I am? invites a response that illuminates what it means to be made 'in the image and likeness of God'.

Early Church Fathers wrote about this 'divinisation' or deification whereby we are drawn into a union with God to *become participants of the divine nature* (2 Peter: 1: 4). There are many statements by early Church Fathers of the Eastern tradition about the theme of theosis or deification such as the following:

Becoming a god is the highest goal of all (St Basil d 379).

God became man so that we might become deified (St Athanasius d 373).

The glory of God is the human person fully alive (St Irenaeus d 202).

Let us seek to be like Christ because Christ also became like us; to become gods through him since he himself, through us, became a man. He took the worst upon himself to make us the gift of the best (Gregory of Nazianzen 390).

The word of God, our Lord Jesus Christ... did through His transcendent Love, become what we are, that He might bring us to be even what He is Himself (St Irenaeus d 202).

Gregory of Nazianzen described the process of deification as like the polishing of a mirror. As the mirror is being polished, the 'Imago Dei' becomes clearer as the divine light is reflected in the mirror.

St Symeon the New Theologian (949 - 1022) wrote this verse about deification:

What I have seen is the totality recapitulated as ONE,
Received not in essence but by participation.
It is just as if you lit a flame from a live flame:
It is the entire flame you receive.

Other references in affirmation of deification include: Ps 82:6; John 10: 34-35; Matthew 5: 48; 2 Corinthians 3:18; I John 3:3: 4:13.

Our nature is human not divine. We are the image of God 'in a sort of indistinct way' (Veli-Matti Karkkainen: 28). The journey of deification or theosis is not denying one's own humanity but being receptive to the Holy Spirit allowing the 'image and likeness of God' to be made more manifest in us. A human being cannot assume God's divine nature of itself but has the potential to be open to participation in the divine life of the Spirit. Christ is the identical image of God.

Now we have to ask ourselves what did the Fathers of the Church mean by the provocative statements given above. The journey of deification is the journey to become more fully human, *created in the image and likeness of God*. To realise more fully what it means to be 'made in the image and likeness of God' is not losing oneself within the Divine Energy but finding one's True Inner Self rather than be seduced by the allure of the Outer False Self. For the Jesuit palaeontologist Teilhard de Chardin (1881-1955), the role of the Christian is to divinise the world in Christ, to 'Christify' the world by our commitment to fostering justice and love. Teilhard called this journey to God in a process of divinisation as 'Christogenesis'. Love is the driving impulse which will make all this happen.

Sin diminishes this image. Grace restores and enhances the *image and likeness* of God. The word 'sin' is derived from the Old High German word 'sunda' meaning 'to sunder' or 'to tear apart'. Sin is breaking down the inner orientation towards a unity with a God of love. Sin is a diminution of the *image and likeness* of God within us and within our social world.

Through his life, death and resurrection, Christians believe that Jesus as the Christ redeemed our brokenness and moved us towards a union with God. Redemption in Christ is not making up for any primal sin of Adam and Eve but a progression towards a more profound union with God in love. Through forgiveness of sin we are transformed into a new communion with God. The deepest yearning of the human heart is union with the divine, the Source of all being. The mission of Jesus was to fan the spark of divinity within us into a blazing furnace of love, *I came to bring fire to the earth, and how I wish it were already kindled* (Luke 12:49). Christian belief holds that Jesus came to highlight how we are both human and possess something of the divinity in our DNA, created 'in the image and likeness of God'. His mission of teaching about the reign of God explained how this beautiful vision of our humanity and creation might be nurtured and better realised.

> What is your understanding of 'deification'? How does the concept of 'deification' align with the essence of your Christian faith?
>
> Do you consider the notion of 'deification' would help Christians in deepening their faith life? What might be difficult for Christians to accept a 'deification' orientation in the practice of their faith?

Two complementary Christian stories

In the discussions about the two Christian Stories, we are not describing two Christian Stories that are co-existent spiritual allies. Both stories are complementary sacred stories sharing the same fundamental truths about God's revelation in Jesus as the Christ.

The Fall/Redemption Traditional Christian Story emphasises the RESTORATION of the human condition in Christ because of a primal failure by humans.

The Cosmic Christian Story emphasises REGENERATION in Christ within an evolutionary movement in creation towards an emerging unitive consciousness of love.

For those Christians who experience the Cosmic Christian Story as attuned to their own spiritual journeys, what are the implications for Christian living?

Conclusion

This chapter has reflected on the salient features of the Cosmic Christian Story.

The next chapter will explore key themes in the daily living of the Cosmic Christian Story.

Chapter Six

Daily living the Cosmic Christian Story

> *We must remember that it is not only the human world that is held securely in this sacred enfoldment but the entire planet. We need this security, this presence throughout our lives. The sacred is that which evokes the depths of wonder. We may know some things, but really we know only the shadow of things. We go to the sea at night and stand along the shore. We listen to the urgent roll of the waves reaching higher until they reach their limits and can go no farther, then return to an inward peace until the moon calls again for their presence on these shores.*
> *So it is with the fulfilling vision that we may attain – for a brief moment. Then it is gone, only to return again in the deepening awareness of a presence that holds all things together.*
>
> Thomas Berry *The World of Wonder* in 'Spiritual Ecology: The Cry of the Earth', 22.

This chapter discusses core themes in a Cosmic Christian Story and their implications for Christian living. In a certain sense, these themes are common to all Christian living. The difference between the Traditional Christian Story and the Cosmic Christian Story is related to the original impulses for the Incarnation. In the Traditional Christian Story, the original impulse is a restoration mission by Jesus to reconcile humanity with God after the sin of Adam and Eve. In the Cosmic Christian Story, the primal impulse is situating the mission of Jesus as the Christ within the overarching story of the universe.

What does the Cosmic Christian Story look like in daily living?

Once again, we return to themes in modern science already described, which offer possible paths for living the Christian faith according to the Cosmic Christian Story. Each section in this chapter reflects features of our contemporary world that capture some of the spirit of living in this epoch of consciousness.

Cosmic context

The starting point for living the Cosmic Christian story is the recognition and awareness that we live on a small planet within immense galaxies. Our existence as humans has evolved over billions of years from the primal burst of energy 13.7 billion years ago.

Who am I in this wondrous universe?
Every day we engage in the normal activities of living, work, leisure, caring for family, coping with sickness, enjoying good health and so on. The history of religions again and again illustrates how readily religions so contract their numinous vision that these religions all too often formulate rules about not eating from a plate that has been used by non-believers or declaring breaking a fast as a sin. A Zen saying is instructive, 'The wise man points to the moon; the fool studies his fingers'. In the Cosmic Christian Story, Christians are urged never to forget that their very existence has originated within this amazing universe, so vast that its expanse is beyond our comprehension. The psalmist sings, *When I look at your heavens, the work of your fingers, the moon and the stars that you have established* (8:3).

A modern understanding of evolution has changed our understanding of how life develops. Evolutionary science explains how life changes in increasing complexity. The unfolding of life is not just in biology but in every facet of life in the universe. For thousands of years, the static fixed universe of the Greek astronomer Ptolemy was an accepted truth, assuming the earth was the centre of the universe. Copernicus and Galileo disproved Ptolemy's model of the universe. They demonstrated that the earth is a planet rotating around the sun within a bewildering constellation of planets.

The science of emergence demonstrates how new configurations of life arise out of previous forms but not constituted by elements in these forms. New properties are formed to introduce other genres of life that do not possess characters of previous life. The process of emergence enables a wide diversity of life forms to spread across the world without the limitations of being constrained by previous configurations of life. The science of emergence is a hopeful one because it raises all kinds of possibilities for new creations. For Christians and indeed for all religions, the science of emergence provocatively suggests how Divine revelations may assume new and exciting forms within a new paradigm of consciousness. Alternative complementary orthodoxies for Christianity will emerge in succeeding stages of world consciousness because the Spirit is present within the unfolding dynamics of creation. Historians of theology point out how Aquinas in the 13th century used Aristotelian categories to construct his great theological work, the *Summa*. Why should theologians today be reluctant to construct a new theological cosmic framework as an alternative orthodoxy in Christology?

In 1929, the scientist Edwin Hubble (1889 -1953) found that the universe was rapidly expanding. We are not living in a closed universe but one that is growing. The prospect of many universes is now a possibility. Perhaps there may be life on other planets. However the prospect of finding life on these planets is bleak. One light-year equals about 9.5 trillions of kilometres. Potentially habitable planets are likely to be found 11 light years away. Currently no technology exists that would make this journey possible.

The vastness of our universe is almost incomprehensible. It would take a space traveller millions of light years to traverse our universe. Any reflection on the Christian Story apart from its context within the Great Story of the universe leaves the Christian Story without its origins in the outburst of divine Energy, the Source of all being and life. For a religious person, creation did not happen out of nothing ('ex nihilo') but out of the energy explosion of the creative Spirit. From a religious perspective, creation is the outpouring fruit of the 'substance' of God. A theological framework that does not embrace the immensity of the universe and the evolution of all life on our planet limits the cosmic depth of the Incarnation. The elements that constitute our bodies (including the body of Jesus) have originated during the billions of evolutionary years. We all breathe the same air and drink the same water that is prevalent in earth's story. Human bodies are more than 70% constituted by water. Belief in the mystery of the Incarnation suggests that we cannot separate Christ from the cosmic context of God's revelation in Christ.

An evolutionary perspective on the Christ story appreciates how the Christ story is in a process of ongoing development. God is beyond the world and yet within its creative Spirit energy. Those who live the Cosmic Christian Story attend with a listening heart to the pulse of the world about them. As citizens of the earth, we learn to reverence its mysteries and live within the rhythms of nature. The Book of Job expresses this affinity with nature by heeding his advice: *But ask the animals, and they will teach you; the birds of the air, and they will tell you; ask the plants of the earth, and they will teach you; and the fish of the sea will declare to you* (Job 12: 7- 8). As cosmic citizens, we learn to live in awe at the wonder and abundance of life. The sunsets and sunrises, forests and animals, mountains and rivers, the colours of the

Bird of Paradise, all are manifestations of an exotic divine creativity. We also weep with the sufferings of a broken world, not just the consequences of natural disasters but the famines, environmental vandalism, wars and mayhem caused by wicked people and corporate greed. Let nature be our wise teacher.

Relationality

A basic feature of living the Cosmic Christian Story is an awareness of the relationships of everything in the universe. The concept of relationality has been explained previously. Relationality is an intrinsic element in our DNA. The biologist Richard Dawkins popularised the notion of the selfish gene which drives and controls all behaviour according to survival and self-perpetuation. However there is a growing interest in an alternate view according to the field of *epigenetics*. The science of epigenetics posits that genes do not control our lives but that our values, emotions, attitudes and beliefs have a major impact on our genetic code (O'Murchu 2012:156). In the theory of epigenetics, the environment around the cells plays a major role in how the genes work inside the cells. Epigenetics is a much more positive view of our anthropology than those of the deterministic and mechanistic theories of Dawkins. The notion of the genial gene developed by the biologist Joan Roughgarden (2009) aptly designates beliefs about the prospect of our participation in evolving human wisdom. Through our nature as a rational being, we can change the quality of life in the world. We can enhance relationships and communities. We can make a difference. We are not simply victims of chance and blind fate. According to research about epigenetics, we can generate positive energy to people around us by our very presence, our smiles and our welcoming attitudes (Church: 32).

For faith orientated people, a gracious and intimate God invites everyone into a union of love and sharing this love. The presence of relationality and connectedness is the energy of love: *God is love, and those who abide in love, abide in God, and God abides in them* (1 John 4:17). The awareness of universal relationality and the impelling energy of God's love demand a response: *Beloved, let us love one another, because love is from God; everyone who loves is born of God and knows God. Whoever does not love does not know God for God is love* (1 John 4: 7-8). One of the most heartfelt passages in the New Testament is the description of love in Paul's letter to the Corinthians: *Love is patient; love is kind; love is not envious or boastful or arrogant or rude. It does not insist on its own way; it is not irritable* or resentful; it does not rejoice in wrongdoing, but rejoices in the truth (1 Corinthians 13: 4-6). A Cosmic Christian spirituality will emphasise the potential and power of love as the basic energy driving the movement to higher levels of consciousness. Our prayers for others travel across space and time through connecting energy fields. True love is communal in its scope. According to Thomas Aquinas, *amor est diffusivum sui* ('love spreads itself out everywhere').

Suggest how relationality may be lived in everyday life. How would you describe 'love'?

Respect and promotion of life in abundance

If people are created in the 'image and likeness of God' then every single person - regardless of race, religion or social status - is worthy of respect. Wars, racial discrimination, domestic violence, malnutrition, homelessness, poverty all cry out for moral condemnation and direct action. Thousands of children die each day from preventable diseases. The International Labour Organisation estimates that 168 million children are working around the world, many of them working in jobs that are detrimental to their health. Millions of refugees barely survive in camps. Respect for life embraces life in all its forms in creation. *Life in abundance* (John 10:10) is a mantra for all people, including Christians, to support every social or religious movement that promotes fairness and justice. We find God, not in some distant heaven, but standing right there in front of us as, perhaps the person who has no food or home or is an asylum seeker or confronting the trashing of the environment. According to a Sufi saying, 'Wheresoever you turn, there is the face of God'.

As soon as Jesus began his ministry, he went about the countryside healing lepers (Mark 1: 40 - 42), the blind (Mark 8:22-27), exorcism (Mark 5:1-13), the lame (John 5:1-18) and all those afflicted with various disabilities. For Jesus, what was broken must be restored. People must be brought into wholeness, not just physically but spiritually. Readers of the gospels know that we have no eye witness evidence about the physical aspects of the miracles performed by Jesus. What Christians accept is that every miracle story is a cry for people to become whole in body and spirit. The quest for justice can never be an option for any Christian but an imperative for restorative action (Matthew 25:31-46). The array of justice services by the Christian community throughout the world over the centuries gives testimony to a commitment for justice as the essence of the Christian story.

All the great religious traditions have a strong commitment to justice. One of the Five Pillars of Islam is the third Pillar of *Zakat* (giving) which is support of the needy. In Hinduism, Buddhism, Jainism and Sikhism, *Dana* is the virtue of generosity or charity.

The theme of 'abundance' is a repetitive theme in the scriptures. The scriptures regularly speak about a God of abundance not a deity of scarcity. When Moses struck the rock water 'came out abundantly' (Number 20:11). Isaiah describes the abundance of God at the end of the world: *On this mountain, the Lord of hosts will make for all peoples a feast of rich food, a feast of well-aged wines, of rich food filled with marrow, or well-aged wines strained clear* (25:6). In conversation with the Samaritan woman at Jacob's well, Jesus spoke about the abundance of God's grace: *Everyone who drinks of this water will be thirsty again, but those who drink of the water that I will give will never be thirsty. The water that I will give will become in them a spring of water gushing up to eternal life* (John 4:13-14).

Jesus teaches about the abundance of God in the feeding of the five thousand. From a mere five loaves and two fish the whole assembled people ate and yet there were twelve baskets of food left over (Mark 6:30 - 44). There is an abundance of wine at the marriage feast of Cana (John 2). The Last Supper was a sacred ritual meal to give thanks for the abundance of God. The injunction *Do this in remembrance of me* (Luke 22:19) invites all his followers in memory never to limit God's abundance of grace. Grace abounds from a bounteous God (Isaiah 55). The history of religions records how religions have a propensity to confine the scope of grace to their own self-enclosed doctrinal citadels. Currently there is sufficient food and water for the earth's people but its distribution is flawed and wasted through corporate selfishness and corruption.

However, the future of sufficient food is less certain with the population explosion. In the early 1800s, there were one billion people; in 1950, two billion; in 2000, six billion and now 7.4 billion. In 2050, it is estimated that the earth's population will be nine billion. How will the earth's resources cope with the exponential population explosion? Will the abundance of God's bounty for quality living insist on measures to limit the world's population? According to the theory of emergence, will new forms of living patterns appear?

The abundance of life may seem good in theory but do you think it's a realistic idea in the sombre facts of disparity in wealth?

Wisdom and discernment

The image of the Wisdom woman Sophia, partner of the Creator, gazing over the wonder of creation (Proverbs 8:31) is an evocative image for people living in the internet age.

Never before has the human community gained access to so much information. The theoretical physicist Neil Turok presents a startling prediction about the avalanche of information available. He writes, 'And according to Moore's law, in a couple of decades your computer will comfortably hold every single book that has ever been written' (223). With all the information emanating from the internet, does this information have any meaning or does it enhance truth? How do we know what is authentic?

The internet allows worldwide users avenues for instant global communications. Research through the internet is invaluable in terms of time and convenience for acquiring information. Social change is so rapid that many employment opportunities for the younger generation have yet to be invented. Faced with this tsunami of information, it is critical that people learn ways of discernment to make informed choices and resist the dehumanising aspects of social media. Real life situations and reality TV become blurred into one 'reality'. All too often, violence rather than mediation is promoted as the way to resolve conflict. Idealised body images on social media nurture impossible fantasies about the 'perfect body'. In Great Britain, 40% of boys regularly consume pornography and there are 107 million monthly visitors to adult websites in the USA. The ideology of consumerism promotes an insatiable desire for material things. How do people learn to navigate moral paths through siren voices of consumerism? Sophia wisdom instructs us about choosing life: *For whoever finds me (wisdom) finds life and obtains favour from the Lord* (Proverbs 8:35).

In the digital age, the church no longer controls information flows to its members. Google gives access to any topic or any historical contention. Any official church narrative must be scrupulous in its truthfulness if the church is to be credible. There must be transparency in church leadership. Investigative journalism will uncover every religious abuse in the public arena. Values of discipleship will undermine any 'command - obey' official church attitudes unless the teachings are credible in the eyes of church members. Baptism as a sacrament calls all baptised into the discipleship of the People of God. The ancient tradition of *sensus fidelium* needs to be reflected in church structures. 'People support what they create' endorses the baptismal right of people to have some significant investment in how the church functions and makes decisions. There is nowhere to hide in the digital age.

The Hindu practice of painting a third eye (*bindi*) is a symbol of seeing the truth that is beyond delusion. The concept of *maya* (illusion) is very significant in Eastern religions. Through *maya* we can so easily be deluded into thinking external forms are reality. The Buddha's enlightenment under the Bodi Tree was to strip naked delusions of power, wealth and addictions. In Christianity, the venerable tradition of discernment teaches Christians to make decisions in the light of Christ. Regular prayer and meditation are basic ingredients for discernment. The Aborigine leader Miriam-Rose Ungunmerr - Baumann speaks about the concept of *dadirri* or 'inner deep listening'. Inner deep listening assumes a stillness and attentiveness to one's being, the sacredness of the environment and the Spirit Presence.

Sophia, the Wisdom Woman who stands beside the creator, is also a joyous symbol of the Cosmic Christian Story. While acknowledging the genius and service of global technology, we can be overwhelmed by the 24/7 litany of disasters of the world's traumas that fill our screens and airwaves. We join with Sophia in relishing the wonder of creation: *then I was beside him, like a master worker, and I was daily his delight, rejoicing before him always, rejoicing in his inhabited world and delighting in the human race* (Proverbs 8: 30 -31). The spirit of Sophia as a wisdom presence is urgently needed to uncover the deceptions created through manipulation of information through easy digital access and a virtual monopoly of the media by global corporations. Sophia invites us to share the delights of creation and accept responsibility for earth care.

Jesus as the Wisdom Teacher shows a way for wholesome living that fans the flame of the divine image within each person: *Again Jesus spoke to them, saying, 'I am the light of the world. Whoever follows me will never walk in darkness but will have the light of life* (John 8:12).

Why might the symbol of Sophia (the getting of wisdom) be significant in our age of digital technology?

Discuss how the practice of discernment actually happens. What are features of the process of religious discernment?

Oneness

Modern science has verified the essential oneness of all things in creation. The earth is our home and we are beginning learners in creative living as planetary citizens. The Gaia hypothesis of James Lovelock proposed that there is a oneness in the whole of the earth where the biosphere acts like a living organism. Pope Francis in his encyclical *Laudato si* has called for an ecological conversion to the 'Gospel of Creation' (Chapter 2). We are not just inhabitants of the world as passive observers but active earth citizens to transform the world. The age of dualism is surely past where spirit and matter were viewed as separate from one another. In Albert Einstein's theory of relativity, everything is in relationship and everything in the universe is understood to be in relationship with everything else. The Franciscan theologian Ilia Delio writes, 'Just as the physical world is composed of integrally related particles, we too are integrally related to one another and nonhuman creation. We live in a web of relationships, and just as we affect this web by our actions, we too are affected by it' (2011:109).

The early Greek word *katholikos*, meaning 'a sense of wholeness', captures the basic appreciation of the oneness of all things in creation. *Katholikos* brings together cosmology, humanity and divinity into a holistic unity. Modern science tells us that this sense of wholeness is experienced in the interconnectedness of every element in the web of life. The early church adopted the Greek word *catholic* to describe the vision of drawing together all things into a 'wholeness' through Christ. Throughout the centuries the word *catholic* began to lose its original meaning when institutional features of the church began to dominate the model of church. During the second millennium of Christianity the notion of *catholic* assumed the designation of a particular tradition of Christianity often in conflict with other branches of Christianity. An urgent challenge of the Cosmic Christian Story is to restore the primal vision of *katholikos* by confronting sectarianism and promoting a sense of unity and oneness for the whole of creation.

How might we experience 'oneness' in our relationships with nature?

Spirituality

By their very nature, humans are spiritual beings. Spirituality is integral to our DNA. According to St Augustine, 'Oh God, our hearts are restless until they rest in you.' Augustine's haunting words of longing are a refrain that traverses all centuries and religions. In his Confessions, he writes, 'Late have

I loved you, Beauty so very ancient and so ever new. Late have I loved you! You were within, but I was without'. The French philosopher and scientist Blaise Pascal (1623 - 1662) expressed this inner yearning for a Spirit life. According to Pascal, there is within us a 'God-shaped hollow in the human heart that nothing else can fill'.

Spirituality is a personal expression of one's faith. Our own faith life is consoled by the words of Jesus to the woman in Simon's house: *Your faith has saved you; go in peace* (Luke 7:50). There is a hunger in the human heart that is not satisfied with material things. Spirituality is a journey towards encountering God with the heart not just with the mind. Palaeontologists have uncovered abundant evidence to illustrate how ancient peoples sought to connect with the divine spirits in their world. A basic impulse for spirituality is the human longing for meaning and purpose in life. Neuroscience has confirmed that the brain does possess a quality which relates to ultimate questions of values and meaning (Newberg). The word 'holy' is from the Anglo-Saxon word 'hale' meaning 'health'. To engage in a spiritual quest is to seek to become more 'holy' and 'healthy'.

For a theist, the meaning of spirituality is related to one's relationships with a divine Presence or God. A person's spirituality begins with an awareness of God's presence about her or him. A faith filled vision is attentive to how one may find the divine Presence in every nook and cranny of life. Through prayer, we move beyond illusions and encounter God in the reality of our inner being. The medieval mystic Mechthild of Magdeberg (1210 - 1282) expressed this encountering God as a convergence towards the Source of being:

> Each creature God made
>
> Must live in its own true nature,
>
> How could I resist my nature,
>
> That lives for oneness with God?

How people image God or a divine Presence is a vital aspect of their spirituality. God is incomprehensible. Paul warns us that: *for now we see in a mirror, dimly* (1 Corinthians 13: 12). St Augustine named this paradox about knowing God, 'If you have understood, it is not God' (*Sermon* 117.5). The image of the 'God-out-there' who from time to time intervenes in human affairs suggests that God is apart and beyond everyday happenings. The intervention god may be called upon to ensure fine weather for the parish fair or to help the home team win a football match. All too often, a god image considered god as a supernatural bookkeeper who kept a careful audit of good and bad deeds to be revealed on Judgment Day.

The rich traditions of the church in spirituality through time-honoured devotions, prayers, Eucharist, sacraments, scriptures, ascetical practices and pilgrimages provide deep wells of spiritual wisdoms. The practice of *Lectio divina* ('divine reading') describes an approach to reading scripture in a prayerful way, either individually or in community. The Eucharist has a central place in Christian worship and prayer. The 'Jesus prayer' is an ancient venerable mantra. A Cosmic spirituality will drink from the spiritual reservoirs of other religious and indigenous traditions and practices. The wisdoms of Jewish mysticism in Kabbalah, Sufi mysticism of Islam, the Vedas of Hinduism and the Four Noble Truths of Buddhism, all offer enriching spiritualities that are diverse but universal for all traditions.

Eco-spirituality connects us with the Spirit who impregnates all nature. One of the influential contemporary movements in spirituality is reclaiming the natural world in the scope of Christian spirituality. Pope Francis in *Laudato si* (2015) speaks about 'The Gospel of Creation' in Section Two of the encyclical. Note the power of the word 'gospel'. Early Christian spirituality was deeply affected by the Gnostic dualism of spirit=good, material= evil. Neo-Platonic dualism advocated leaving behind material things and ascending to Plato's Eternal Forms. Only in more recent times has Christianity begun to shake off its inherited dualism that disdained bodily and earthly things. I recall the resistance in ecumenical groups to any prospect of my doing tai'chi for relaxation and burning a calming oil such as lavender. Natural wisdoms of spirituality expressed in such areas as aromatherapy and tai'chi tend to be regarded with suspicion by some evangelical groups as somehow diminishing the Christ above nature.

Eco-spirituality is not some romantic tree-hugging experience but proactive action in trying to reverse the downward spiral of threats to the biosphere. The notion of 'kinship' rather than 'stewardship' captures our relationships, not just our ethical responsibilities, in our living styles as citizens of the earth community. That 25% of the earth's population use 75% of the earth's resources is surely a matter of grave concern to all who uphold a kinship with the earth community. That 69 wealthy people in the world own half the wealth of 3.5 billion people is nothing short of a serious aberration of the common good.

Eco-spirituality begins in a sense of awe and wonder of the marvel of God's creation in its biodiversity. In the rush of scheduled tyrannies of modern life, we may fail to notice the painted skies of a sunrise or sunset. The iPad screen far too readily becomes the substitute for the 'screen' of the flowering garden. The latest Facebook communication replaces nature's communication of a morning song chorus by birds. To stand and gaze on an orchid garden is to enter a sacred world of intricate colours. To walk in a forest is to wander down the aisles of nature's cathedral. Forest therapy is recommended for psychological healing. The discovery of drugs from nature reminds us of the healing power of nature. The aspirin, for example, was developed from the bark of willow trees. We easily become no longer beholders of creation's wonders but victims of technological addictions. The Roy Morgan study of more than 9000 Australians (2016) found that half claimed that they can no longer live without their smartphones. The majority of the world's population lives in cities with little or no direct contact at all with the natural world. Their feet walk on pavements but hardly ever on soil. Teachers who take inner city children on excursions are often stunned to find students who do not know that milk comes from cows.

A prayerful meditation by Thomas Moore is also a parable about learning to attend to environmental treasures all around us:

> A pilgrim was walking a long road when one day he passed what seemed to be a monk sitting in a field. Nearby, men were working on a stone building.
> 'You look like a monk,' the pilgrim said.
> 'I am that,' said the monk.
> 'Who is that working on the abbey?'
> 'My monks,' said the man. 'I'm the abbot.'
> 'It's good to see a monastery going up,' said the pilgrim.
> 'They are tearing it down,' said the abbot.
> 'Whatever for?' asked the pilgrim.
> 'So we can see the sun rise at dawn,' said the abbot.
>
> Moore, Thomas, *Meditations: On the Monk Who Dwells in Daily Life*, New York. Harper Collins Publishers, 1994).

What 'walls' do we need to tear down to see and appreciate the grandeur of nature, its beauty and its fury?

A feature of contemporary movements in religion today is turning away from institutional forms of religion to seek a spirituality that embraces all aspects of life. Such a trend is a feature of a general rejection of institutions such as governments and churches. Current world politics shows how deep are the public alienation to governments, bureaucracy and authority. There is a growing desire to pursue deep inner impulses authenticating their own life experiences. A direct personal communications with a Divine Presence can bypass the need for mediation through ecclesiastical institutions or religious intermediaries.

What signs (if any) do you notice of changing patterns of spirituality among people?

Authentic Christian community

We are relational and communal by nature. An autonomous Christian is a contradiction in terms. Our inner being craves love, intimacy, friends, families and communities. To be in union with God is to share the intimacy of God's love: *God is love, and those who abide in love abide in God, and God abides in them* (1 John 4:16). As relational sexual people, we are all part of each other's lives. The early Christian communities were formed as a sign of a radical, egalitarian, new way of fellowship (agape) in sharing the Good News of the reign of God. The ideal of community is expressed by St Paul, *For just as the body is one and has many members, and all the members of the body, though many, are one body, so it is with Christ. For in the one Spirit, were all baptised into one body – Jews or Greeks, slaves or free – and we were all made to drink of the one Spirit* (I Corinthians 12:12-13). The idealised community is quite different from the reality of a daily living of imperfect communities with their sharing, conflicts, generosity, ethnic diversity, pastoral services and worship.

Paul reminds us that there are many gifts of the Spirit in the community and the sharing of these gifts will enhance the wellbeing of the community: *Now there are varieties of gifts, but the same Spirit...To each is given the manifestation of the Spirit for the common good* (1 Corinthians 12: 4,7). In community, members worship together and celebrate what the Good News means in everyday life. Everyone in the community has some birth-gift to make a difference to people's lives and the earth community.

The Eucharist is the focus of the assembled community. The injunction of Jesus at the last Supper, *Do this in remembrance of me* (Luke 22:20) invites the Christian community in faith to allow the eternal Christ to be present through the transformation of the daily bread and blood of life into a living Presence. The communal ritual meal of the Eucharist celebrates the union of love with God, the gathered people and the fruits of creation, bread and wine. The Eucharist is an act of deification by the worshiping community whereby the 'image and likeness of God' becomes more realised through worship and consuming the sacred bread and wine. Sacraments are special communal signs of God's grace. Each sacrament is a ritual, leading Christians towards the life journey of a further participation in deification.

In his ministry, Jesus devoted much of his time to teaching about community. Leadership in the community is one of service not of power over others (Mark 10: 43). Relations among members of community affirm value differences but insist on forgiveness and reconciliation. A Christ community is committed to proactive service for those in need. Being a member of a community involves personal investment in community relationships. Authentic communities have members who are especially vulnerable and fragile. Such members are precious reminders of God's mercy and compassion through the love and care that they receive in an inclusive community.

The family is the primary community as the 'domestic church'. In the Apostolic Exhortation *Amoris Laetitia* ('The Joy of Love') 19th March 2016, Pope Francis has urged that everything should be done to enhance the quality and protection of family life. The complexity of family life situations, cultural differences and legal specifications make pastoral care of families very difficult. Questions that arise in such areas as divorce, blended families, custody tensions, families with disabilities, ethnic customs, same sex unions, all invite compassionate and pastoral responses. Life enhancing parishes and devotional groups are sources of support and evangelisation. The Christian community is a service community for promoting justice and peace in the world.

If the church is to be an authentic community for its members, it must undergo a serious reformation of its structures of governance. The current disengagement of members from their Christian communities will not be reversed unless the *sensus fidelium* is honoured in practice. The current structures of the church reflect the last vestiges of a closed feudal medieval system that is quite dysfunctional and bypasses accountability and participation. The culture of clericalism is a major impediment to authentic church renewal. Pope Francis has denounced clericalism as 'one of the greatest deformations' in the church.

The Jesus vision of community is egalitarian in its character and contradicts a domination model of leadership. Most Christians know that in reality they have no real say in what happens in how the Church functions or what it teaches. The proclamation of *Humanae Vitae* (1968) ignored the recommendation for change in teachings on birth control by 57 of the 61 members of the commission. The deciding factor ultimately came down to the preservation of the papal teaching of Pope Pius XI in *Casti Connubii*, 1931 (n 53-62). One could list a depressingly long series of prophetic voices in the church that have been and are now, silenced or marginalised. Until church structures encourage sacred spaces for informed conversations and discernment of the Spirit, lasting renewal will always struggle against the prevailing winds of conservatism. How will the Spirit break open the closed system of the church?

Early in the life of the *ecclesia* (Greek for 'gathering'), there emerged governance structures which drew from Jewish and Greek models. We read of *episkopos* or 'overseers' or 'guardians' (bishops), deacons, deaconesses and a whole array of diverse ministries.

The top-downwards culture, rather than the current hierarchical structure in the church, is a heritage of the writings of a fifth-century writer Pseudo-Dionysius who expounded the notion of two sacred divinely constituted orders, the Celestial or Angelic Hierarchy (Seraphim, Cherubim, Thrones, Dominations, Archangels, Angels) and the Ecclesiastical Hierarchy which designates a descending order from bishops, priests, deacons, monks and laity. The Dionysian Hierarchy mirrored the three-tiered fixed universe of Ptolomy that reflected God's fixed order for harmony in the world and church. The apex of the order was more perfect in quality than the lower order of monks and laity. The enterprise of transforming the passive role of the laity to active participants in the life of the church, including ministry and leadership, has to overcome a thousand year old tradition of upholding a purported divine descending/ascending plan for church governance and accountability. One of the reasons for the non-ordination of women as stated in *Ordinatio Sacerdotalis* (1994) is that the exclusion of women is in accord with God's fixed hierarchical plan for the church.

An authentic Christian community is not an incestuous cult of like-minded believers but an imperfect evangelising community reaching out to share the Good News of transformation for 'life in abundance'. Good Christian communities assist people to connect with one another by sharing the God story in Jesus and the marvel of the universe story.

To what extent is belonging to a Christian community a significant feature of your Christian faith?

From your experiences of belonging to a Christian community, what learnings can you share about what is helpful/ not helpful in Christian communities?

Inclusion and women

The question of the full inclusion of women in the life of the church merits a more detailed discussion than other themes discussed previously. The inclusion of women in church structures and culture raises wider questions about the nature of the church itself and a holistic anthropology. The growing movement towards fostering a holistic anthropology underpins many of the dilemmas raised in earlier chapters that relate to the development of an alternative orthodoxy in the Cosmic Christian Story. The question, *Who do you say I am?* asked by Jesus about his identity is also the core question for each one of us, *Who do you say I am?* Who am I as a sexual being? The issue of women and inclusion in church cannot be answered apart from wider global questions about women in society and our understanding of the sexual nature of the human person.

From earliest times, feminine expressions of divinity were common in most indigenous and religious cultures. The Great Mother Goddess was a symbol of earth fertility and the archetypal feminine symbol in the collective unconscious of humanity. Feminine divinities represented creative energy in creation, mother of all living things on earth and the symbol of life. In Babylon and Assyria, the goddess was Ishar; in Egypt she was Isis; in Syria and Palestine there were goddess such as Demeter, Astarte and Hera, all Earth Mothers and symbols of fertility. Seeds are the source of growth and life. Throughout history, women were the seed keepers and the sacredness of the seed was symbolised by images of mother goddesses. In Christian piety, one perspective on Marian devotion was that the Virgin Mother expressed the archetypal symbol of fertility and life. As the Christian community expanded across the globe, the question of the feminine principle of fertility and holistic sexuality has struggled to find a healthy integration into the institutional system of the church and its teachings on sexuality.

One of the contributing factors in the dominance of misogyny in Western culture is explained by Richard Tarnas: 'Many generalisations could be made about the history of the Western mind, but today perhaps the immediately obvious one is that it has been from start to finish an overwhelmingly masculine phenomenon: Socrates, Plato, Aristotle, Paul, Augustine, Aquinas, Luther, Copernicus, Galileo, Bacon, Descartes, Newton, Locke, Hume, Kant, Darwin, Marx, Nietzsche, Freud.... The Western intellectual tradition has been produced and canonised entirely by men, and informed mainly by male perspectives' (441). During the last half century, feminist writings have begun to correct this massive gender bias in Western intellectual tradition. The feminist contribution to a holistic anthropology has not yet significantly impacted on church life and governance although the emergence of women theologians is beginning to address the male bias in official church life and theology. Theologians such as Elizabeth Johnson, describe the link between the exploitation of the earth and the subordinate status of women in history (1993:10).

The full participation of women in every level of church life is a basic principle in an alternative orthodoxy of the Christian faith. The static prohibition against women's status and ordination without any coherent rationale based on modern scriptural scholarship and holistic anthropology reflects a closed system. A desired aspiration of the church as an open system shows how discerned change would bring new life to the Christian community.

Sooner or later, some Christian churches, such as the Catholic and Orthodox Church, must face the question of full inclusion of women in all levels of governance and ministries including the diaconate and ordination of women. To fail to do so will marginalise the Church even further from cultural relevance and contradict the inclusion of oneness in God's providence.

God is beyond gender. Any exclusion of women from full participation in the life of the church is an historically conditioned cultural phenomenon rather than any assumption of knowing the mind of God. Patriarchy is an affront to God's vision for wholeness in humanity. Entrenched patriarchy will not be overcome by legislation alone. There needs to be a conversion of the heart that sees women and men in the fullness of their female and male sexuality as created 'in the image and likeness of God'. A woman cannot be regarded as some kind of honorary man.

The feminist movement in today's world goes to the heart of being human in contemporary culture. The feminist movement critiques societal assumptions about the respective roles of men and women, the dominance of patriarchy and sexism in all its forms. The issue of equity of women in the world is much more urgent than women's status in the church life. Gender discrimination is a world-wide problem of entrenched patriarchy and the enforced legal inferior status of woman. Domestic violence, human trafficking, genital mutilation, arranged marriages, inequity in wages and social subordination are just some of the more obvious expressions of the subjugation of basic rights for women. An Indian laywoman, Dr Astrid Lobo Gajiwala, who has collaborated with the Catholic Bishops Conference of India, is reported as saying, 'For me it is about women in poverty – Indian women, who literally have second class status with little or no access to education or healthcare. We have the highest maternal mortality rate in the world but we also have a declining sex ratio.... The reason is that the girl child is killed off.'(quoted in *The Tablet* 2 May 2015 9).

The inferior status of women has an enduring history in antiquity and is prevalent in most cultures. The inferior status of women has its origins in a cultural history that is related to purity regulations, economic roles and blood issues in menstruation. The Sumerian civilisation bequeathed to humanity many inventions we take for granted such as writing, the wheel and mathematics. However, the Sumerian legal code declared, 'If a woman speaks out of turn, her teeth shall be smashed with a brick'. Greek and Roman authors were at one in according an inferior status of women in society and governance. By the fifth century, ancient Greece required all women to wear different kinds of veils denoting to observers their different status.

Western and later Christian attitudes towards women were also shaped by Aristotle's physiology which Thomas Aquinas endorsed. Thomas wrote in the *Summa*, 'In terms of nature's own operation, a woman is inferior and a mistake' (ST 1 q 92, 1 ad 1). In Aristotle's physiology, the male seed is the formal cause of conception whereas the woman is only the material passive cause of conception. When a female is conceived, she is actually a failed male. Aristotle's physiology was passed into the Eastern Church through Clement of Alexandria (c 150 - c 215) and the Western church through Tertullian (c 155 – c 220). Misogynist attitudes in Christianity were reinforced by a biblical literalism of blaming Eve the temptress for the first sin. Tertullian described Eve as 'the gateway through which the devil comes'.

Greek and Roman heritage shaped Christian thinking. Albert the Great, the teacher of Thomas Aquinas, taught that, 'Woman is a misbegotten man and has a faulty and defective nature in comparison with his' (Albertus Magnus, *Commentary on Aristotle's "Animals"* 15, q.11).

The misogynist structures of the church insulate celibate church leaders and some theologians from the day-to-day significant relations with women. In recent times a growing number of women theologians are enriching theology through a feminist perspective. There are libraries of resources composed by men (not women) about whom women were and are now. The final vote at the Synod on the Family in October 2015 was a vote by over 200 celibate males. That comment is no reflection on the wisdom and integrity of the bishops who were present, simply a reflection of the paucity of church structures where a topic involving family life is finally voted on by clerics who are not daily participants in family life. Until the structures of the Catholic Church are modified on gender equity, little will happen to erode an entrenched patriarchy.

The prohibition against ordination of women as deacons and priests is understandable in its historical context. However, from the perspective of our historical knowledge about the cultural sources of patriarchy, it is disturbing to note the continued resistance by the official Catholic Church to the full incorporation of women into the life of the church. In the light of modern biblical studies and emerging cultural gender equity, especially in Western countries, the current exclusion of women from hierarchical roles such as the diaconate and ordination itself has no credible rationale except claims for upholding a time-bound ecclesial tradition. In a growing consciousness about gender equity and women exercising leadership now in all dimensions of public life such as commerce, politics, military, social services, local governance, why would it seem to be God's will to exclude women from the one area of liturgical leadership?

Let us consider some themes pertinent to the full incorporation of women into all levels of church life including ministry and governance:

1. In the life of Jesus, we read how his ministry and teachings involved women as disciples. He mixed with women who were prostitutes, explained his mission with a Samaritan woman (John 4) and included women in his travelling ministry as disciples. Women followers of Jesus accompanied him from Galilee to Jerusalem (Luke 23: 49). Women stayed with Jesus to the bitter end of his crucifixion (John 19:25-27; Matthew 27:55; Luke 23:27; Mark 15:40). Mary Magdalene was commissioned by Jesus to announce the glorious news of the resurrection (John 20:17). In the early church, Mary Magdalene was called 'the apostle to the apostles'.

2. The ideal of inclusion in Christ is succinctly expressed in Galatians, *There is no longer Jew or Greek, there is no longer slave or free, there is no longer male and female; for all of you are one in Christ Jesus* (3:28).

3. There are many examples of the critical role of women in early Christianity. Junia, a woman, is an apostle (Romans 16:7). There are five mission teams of twos that have women in them, Prisca and Aquila (Romans 16:30), Andronicus and Junia (Romans 16:7), Philologus and Julia (16:15), Nereus and his sister (16:15), Euodia and Syntyche (Philippians 4:2-3). Nympha was a leader in a house church (Colossians 4:15). In the early writing *The Shepherd of Hermes* (148 CE), Grapte and Clement are mentioned as female and male church leaders.

4. A consensus opinion among scripture scholars is that there was no such a thing as a rite of ordination at the Last Supper as the rite of ordination is understood today. The Twelve represented the leaders of the Twelve Tribes of the new Israel for the inauguration of the Kingdom. We read of many ministries in the early church such as miracle workers, prophets, teachers, evangelists, tongue-speakers and interpreters, elders, healers and workers for the gospel. We do not read of any ministry specific to leadership of the Eucharist. Women were very active in the life of early Christian communities. Since baptism in the early church involved immersion of naked candidates for baptism, women leaders carried out the immersion of women in the first phase of the baptism ritual. Deaconesses were

active in the early church (1 Timothy 3:11). Phoebe was a 'deacon' and 'leader' of the church in Cenchreae (Romans 16:1-2).

5. There are several references to women as deacons in the first three centuries. The third century *Didascalia Apostolorum* ('Teaching of the Apostles') gives instruction to men and women who are deacons. The theologian Origen (185-253), in his commentary of Phoebe as deacon, writes, '... that there are, as we have already said, women deacons in the church, and that women, who by their good works, deserve to be praised by the apostle, ought to be accepted in the diaconate'. Sophia in the second half of the 4th century is a deacon; Maria a deacon in the 6th century. In the Eastern churches, deaconesses were active as late as the 12th and 13th centuries. A ritual of sacramental ordination for women deacons is noted in the Council of Chalcedon (451). A majority of scholars agree that for almost the first half of Christian history, the role of women as deacons was sanctioned by scripture and had apostolic foundations (Macy, G. Ditewig, W. & Zagano, P. 11).

6. We read about the priesthood of the whole Christian community (1 Peter 2:5) but not any mention of individual priests. It would appear that whoever was the community leader was the leader of the Eucharist. Since some women were community leaders, there would seem to be a reasonable deduction that women sometimes led the Eucharist celebration. The theologian Edward Schillebeeckx sums up the Eucharistic leadership position in the early church, 'Thus the general conception is that anyone who is competent to lead the community in one way or another is *ipso facto* also president of the Eucharist (and in this sense presiding at the Eucharist does not need any separate authorisation)' (Schillebeeckx: 30).

7. Historically it is important not to confuse apostles with the Twelve. The Twelve represented symbolically the twelve tribes of the New Israel. Apostles (meaning 'one who is sent') or emissaries preached the gospel in a travelling ministry. Paul, Barnabas and Junia (a woman) were not of the Twelve but were apostles.

8. As the church continued to grow, structures began to take shape and these structures were influenced by the cultural environment as a mix between Jewish, Roman and Greek misogynist views about

women. Restrictive practices against women soon began to appear as reflecting prevailing cultural attitudes. For example, in Roman society women could not hold public office. Writings by the church Fathers from the third centuries onwards illustrate how quickly patriarchy became the established norm in church ministries and structure. Women were relegated into inferior positions in church mission. Menstruation and childbirth were gradually seen during the fifth and sixth centuries as serious impediments to sanctuary ministry and ordination as deacons, at least in the Western church. The Council of Orange (441) specified that no deaconesses were to be ordained. The Council of Orleans (533) declared against women as deacons 'because of the weakness of the sex' and then later because of 'monthly impurity' (cf Phyllis Zagano : *Women in Ministry*).

9. Apart from deeply entrenched anthropological traditions against women for priesthood, other reasons were proposed for their exclusion. Some of these reasons which have previously been offered as a rationale against the ordination of women almost belie belief. For example, note the biological literalism of the argument ('ionic' representation) which stated that since the priest is in *figura Christi* or in *persona Christi* (in the image of Christ) and since Christ was male, a woman priest could not be a representative of a male Christ – as if every priest has to be an Aramaic speaking circumcised Jew! Also there is the insulting implication that a woman could not be 'another Christ'!

10. The cause of women's ordination is difficult to promote in the Catholic Church because of the official teaching of the magisterium on the issue. However, to insist that the topic of women's ordination is 'closed' because a pope so declared (Pope St John Paul II: *Ordinatio Sacerdotalis* 22nd May 1994) is a dubious argument if the story of historical reversals of papal statements is recorded (cf the Bull of Pope Eugene IV *Cantate Domino* declared that only those in the church could be saved from eternal damnation). A problem for Catholics is that the rationale given for the prohibition of women's ordination in the papal ruling does not withstand serious scrutiny from New Testament scholars and early church historians. The rationale given that the church was founded by men only and that Jesus ordained men is a position held by few (if any?)

scripture scholars. The actual Last Supper accounts in the gospels as studied by scholars avoid any literalism of application to modern celebrations of the Eucharist (see e.g. Chilton, Bruce, *The Eucharist-Exploring its Origins.* Bible Review 10.6 Dec 1994, 36 - 43). The majority of the members of the Pontifical Commission in 1976 concluded that the New Testament by itself alone does not settle the problem of the 'possible accession of women to the presbyterate'.

History is replete with examples of teachings by popes which have been reversed in later centuries. Slavery was not finally condemned by the church until 1890. The argument that 'exclusion of women from the priesthood is in accordance with God's plan for the church' falters if we look at similar statements by popes throughout history that have been modified by later teachings. If the only rationale for the exclusion of women in all levels of church life is an appeal to authority and a historically conditioned tradition, then the movement towards the full incorporation of women in all levels of church life will continue to grow. If one accepts the veracity of *sensus fidelium*, then the topic is very much open for discernment and further scholarship. Research on this topic among Catholics shows a steady increase of people, especially the younger generation, in favour of women's ordination. There are various movements such as Women's Ordination Worldwide (WOW) and Church for Daughters which promote the cause of women's ordination. With an estimated 20% of the 1.2 billion Catholics with no regular access to Sunday Eucharist and the growing movement of merging parishes, the imperative for married priests and ordination of women is a beneficial option. The church cannot keep insisting the Eucharist is 'the source and summit of the Christian life' (*Lumen Gentium* 11) and then prevent 20% of its members from participating in regular Sunday Eucharist by its intransigence in modifying criteria for the presider of the Eucharist.

11. Other Christian traditions, such as the Anglican or Episcopalian church, have not only ordained women as priests but also bishops.
12. There would be many formidable obstacles for the Catholic Church to ordain women, not the least would be relationships with the Orthodox Churches and also in the patriarchal culture of the

emerging churches in African and Asian countries. Ordination of women would have to be preceded by a widespread transforming movement to erode entrenched misogynist national and church cultures. The divisions in the Anglican churches following the ordination of women serve as a warning about the urgency of transforming patriarchal culture.
13. If the only response of the official church to those advocating ordination of women as deacons and priests is an exercise of authority by marginalisation, exclusion and even excommunication, without offering any coherent Christ-driven rationale for the ordination question, then such a response denies a discernment of the Spirit by the People of God.

The full inclusion of women in all levels of church life would serve as a prophetic witness to the whole world as a social statement about gender equity and communal wholeness. Previous biological stereotypes about men and women can no longer be defended. The equal value and dignity of women is an absolute value in our culture. The Church is out of step with this value if it persists in upholding a culture of women's subordination in its ministries and structures.

As the movement towards the full inclusion of women in the life of the church is augmented, this movement should never become a denigration of the sacred ministry of ordination and commitment of priests in their generous service to the mission of the church. Advocacy for the restoration of women as deacons is certainly gathering momentum to reconnect and restore the first traditions of the church for an inclusive diaconate ministry of liturgical, preaching, teaching and compassionate service.

A comprehensive inclusion of women in world cultures, not as subordinates, but as equal partners with males, is a basic element in a holistic appreciation of the oneness in all creation. The gender inclusion movement in the church will simply not go away because it is an expression of the inclusive ministry of Jesus. The warning of Gamaliel to the Council members who were persecuting the first Christians is as relevant today as it was then: *if this plan or undertaking is of human origin it will fail; but if it is of God, you will not be able to overthrow them - in that case you may even be fighting against God* (Acts: 5:38-39).

A Cosmic Christian Story gives witness to this principle of gender equity through its theology, spirituality, governance structures in ministry and pastoral practices. A process of discernment involving the whole People of God will navigate a way forward for how best the reign of God is promoted and lived. The masculine ('animus') and feminine ('anima') are complementary archetypal impulses towards an energy of a divine oneness within the integrity of creation.

> *What has been (is now) your experience of women's role in the church?*
>
> *How do you see the future of women's participation in the life of the church?*

The last things – life journeys beyond death

Death is a door that opens a person to another phase of the trajectory of the life journey. After death, the prospect of 'eternal life' is obviously in the realm of the unknown. Studies on After Death Communications (ADC) exhibit a myriad of experiences by the bereaved such as visionary encounters, conversations, dreams and even a sense of physical contact from departed loved ones (Nowotny-Keane). Space and time dissolve at the point of death. In Christian belief, dying is a spiritual event that marks the sacredness of this passage into a new form of one's life with a different kind of body and a different consciousness. Judaism, Christianity and Islam see the life trajectory as linear, moving horizontally into afterlife.

Most other religions view life after death as transmigration, moving upwards and downwards according to the consequences of how one's life was lived on earth and the karma that one deserves. All religions insist that there are enduring consequences for our worldly actions. In the Hindu tradition as described in the Upanishads, each person has an eternal Self (*Atman*). The Mahayana of Buddhism denies any notion of permanent Self. According to the teachings of the Mahayana, the nature of all things is 'emptiness' (*Shunyata*).

There are obvious difficulties in describing the traditional understandings of the Last Things (Judgment, Purgatory, Heaven and Hell). Apart from the obvious fact that no one has returned to directly report about the Last Things, images of the Last Things have been vividly portrayed in art, visions and literature. The images are both terrifying and consoling. The medieval Italian poet Dante Alighieri's *Divine Comedy* portrayed an epic inferno with demons writhing in torment. I remember my own childhood fear while attending the fiery sermons on hell during parish missions. Modern theology has been slow to discourse on the realm of eschatology (concerned with our final destiny). While the vivid and frightening features of the Last Things have largely dissipated in modern theology, there is some trepidation in venturing into the province of the mystery of 'life' after death. A further difficulty is the enduring dualism of spirit/matter split that is deeply embedded in Christian anthropology and thus reinforces the notion of a spiritual being moving on after death to an eternal destiny of heaven or hell.

For a Christian, beliefs about the Last Things are interwoven with the death and resurrection of Jesus. The resurrection of Jesus is a foundational belief in the Christian faith. Paul is quite explicit: *if Christ has not been raised, then our proclamation has been in vain and your faith has been in vain* (1 Corinthians 15:14). The death and resurrection of Jesus as the Christ is a prototype of our own destiny.

Heaven and hell are not places but states of being within fields of energy. In contradiction to the dualism of Plato and Descartes, quantum physics has revealed how matter and spirit are interconnected bundles of energy. Subatomic particles become forms and are observed when these particles are in relationship to something else. The interconnectedness of all life in the universe suggests that after death the external matter of the body is decomposed while each essential inner human being is transformed into an energy that moves in an evolutionary progression towards a union with the Source of all Energy, God. How this movement happens seems to be related to a facilitation or inhibition according to the quality of love experienced in this life. In traditional language, 'heaven' evokes 'facilitation' towards the Source of Love, whereas 'hell' suggests 'inhibition' or 'estrangement' from reaching this Divine Source of Love. The concept of 'purgatory' relates to the evolutionary process of birth-death-regeneration, the journey towards love. In Tibetan Buddhism, *bardo* is a description of an intermediate state of life between death and rebirth. The state could be a kind of heaven or hell or any state in between, depending on how a person had lived. After-death Christian hope is an aspiration towards an evolutionary convergence of personhood with the Source of Being in a union of love. Heaven is the new creation where love and being are in a state of becoming one. The medieval mystic Meister Eckhart once observed, 'Between a person and God there is no distinction. They are one. Their knowing is with God's knowing. Their activity is with God's activity, their understanding is with God's understanding. The same eye with which I look at God is the eye with which God looks at me'.

No one really knows what happens after death. However, in a Cosmic Christian Story, the passage into eternity, which is beyond space and time, might be described as a more profound realisation of the evolutionary movement towards deification. Such a process of deification is a movement towards a greater realisation of the deepening of the 'image and likeness of God' in each person and a dynamic on-going union with the Source of Being.

Citizens of the Earth

A Cosmic Christian Story reminds Christians that, in the words of Pope Francis, *Our insistence that each human being is an image of God and should not make us overlook the fact that each creature has its own purpose...The entire material universe speaks of God's love, his boundless affection for us* (Laudato si 84). Threats to the earth's biodiversity such as global warming will never be solved by science alone but by a conversion to a reverence for nature. The era of anthropomorphism is over. The emerging sixth great extinction of species must be reversed. This coming epoch is called the 'anthropocene era' because for the first time humans control the planet and determine its future wellbeing. Humans are a unique expression of the evolution of species. Through consciousness, they have a special role in relationships to the environment. In the age of biocentrism, humans must learn to live cooperatively with all other life forms. Permaculture, biodynamic cultivation, organic gardening, holistic farming and utilisation of renewable sources of energy enhance sustainability. Climate change is not a hypothesis but a daily reality of harsh droughts and melting ice caps. Westerners tend to be individualistic and isolationist in their thinking, lacking an appreciation of the interconnectedness of everything in creation.

One of the most misunderstood verses in the Bible - *and fill the earth and subdue it; and have dominion over the fish of the sea and over the birds of the air and over every living thing that moves upon the earth* (Genesis 1:28) - seems to anoint the human species as having lordship over the whole of creation. Instead of a domination mode of relating to the earth, humans are called to a cooperative communal kinship of relationships. Anthropocentrism is to be replaced by cosmocentrism. The uniqueness of the human species is not a rationale for attitudes of control and arrogance. We are utterly dependent on the earth for our very life through oxygen to breathe and food to eat. A growing cosmic awareness is generating social groups to be more active in opposition to corporate industry which is despoiling planetary health. Every single person can do something to enhance environmental care, such as planting trees, water conservation, using solar energy, recycling and supporting neighbourhood environmental groups.

The ethics of eco-theology insist that human attitudes and behaviours towards ecological wellbeing are moral imperatives and not merely green tinted ethical options. Ecocide, the killing of the environment, is a dictum in observing the fifth commandment. Pope Francis has called for an *ecological conversion* (*Laudato si* 216) and that conversion awaits the church and the global commercial world of capitalism. Eco-feminism has introduced valuable insights into environmental ethics by advocating a much more holistic approach to earth care than the previous masculine/domination model of human interaction with nature.

Inter-religious cooperation

An encouraging feature of twenty-first century religion is the growing movement to find common ground between the great religious traditions of Hinduism, Buddhism, Christianity, Islam and Judaism. The trend towards globalism, growing popularity of world travel, internet, threat of terrorism and concerns about the environment are motivating factors in the pursuit of inter-religious cooperation. This inter-faith cooperation tends to bypass the impossible quest of mapping out common doctrinal agreements. That aspiration for common shared doctrinal agreements denies the wisdoms inherent in each religious tradition. Instead of some kind of faux inter-faith orthodoxy, contemporary movements in the inter-faith enterprise seek to discover common ground for a shared spirituality. Such a shared spirituality would affirm common values and enrich the wellbeing of the whole planet through the promotion of harmony and reconciliation. Religions are being urged now to put aside past differences, reject sectarianism and make a commitment to the common good. No one religious tradition of itself can resolve the serious problems now facing the world. A Cosmic Christian Story will only emerge as an authentic orthodoxy if it flourishes within a climate of religious pluralism. Religious exclusivity has no place in a multi-faith world.

The religious heritage of humanity has been enriched by thousands of years of spiritual treasures emanating from a diversity of religions. The sources for religious wisdoms include spiritualities associated with religious expressions such as indigenous sacred rituals, the *Mahayana* or 'Great Vehicle' offering the ideal of the *bodhisatta* or 'future Buddha', the Vedas and Upanishads in Hinduism, Taoism as living in harmony with the Tao, Sufi mysticism in Islam, Hasidic Judaism, Charismatic Pentecostals, Quaker Pietism, Christian monasticism and pilgrimages. Every religious tradition has much to learn from the divine revelations inherent in other sacred stories. The Universal Spirit has moved across all peoples in every age of human history. Only now at this time in our human story have we gained access through globalisation to the wisdoms of the Universal Spirit for all humanity and perhaps recover a sense of the sacred in all life.

Share your experiences of interfaith happenings.

Sabbath and silence of the spirit

Our world is a noisy place. People generally seem uncomfortable with silence. Youth are absorbed with their smartphones even when crossing busy streets! Social commentators report on how younger generations experience a high level of anxiety when they are separated from their digital technology. Research studies reveal how nomophobia (smartphone separation anxiety) is growing, with young people admitting that they became very agitated if they were unable to communicate instantly with family and friends (Iowa State University of Science and Technology 2014 survey). The hubbub of modern life banishes the prospect of listening to the whispers of the gentle Spirit. The capacity to be content with solitude is a critical aspect of befriending one's Inner True Self. The gift of silence is also the invitation to become more aware of others who are hurting, feeling the wind on our face, giving thanks for friends and gazing on a garden flower.

Every religious tradition places great store on meditation. Experiments in neuroscience demonstrate how meditation practices lead to altered states of consciousness (Cannato 116 -118). It is difficult to move to higher levels of consciousness unless one engages in regular prayer and meditation. Sabbath is an invitation to draw back from the absorbing events of daily living and allow the addictions of the ego-self to slip away. The experience of *kenosis* or 'letting go' of the tyranny of subjective life-functions empowers one to listen to the heart beats of the soul. The journey within is the journey from False Self to True Self (Merton 34 - 36). The 'image and likeness of God' resides in True Self. The spirit of *kenosis* is described in Philippians: *who, though he was in the form of God, did not regard equality with God as something to be exploited, but emptied himself, taking the form of a slave* (2:6 -7). The 'emptying' movement sensitises us to the world of wonder all around us and the ultimate meaning of life. Through 'emptying', a Christian learns to allow the True Self to be vulnerable to invitations from an intimate God.

A popular name for the movement of focusing attention today is 'mindfulness'. Mindfulness sessions are very much in vogue today. Rarely do practitioners of mindfulness seem to know the Buddhist and monastic roots of this form of contemplation. In the Buddhist tradition, the Buddha ('Awakened One') is often portrayed as sitting in a serene pose of contemplation. From this experience of mindfulness, the Buddha began his journey in teaching the Buddha's Dharma or 'Four Noble Truths'.

The practice of contemplation is a basic ingredient of works for justice. Social justice activism which is not grounded in contemplation too readily descends into projections of power over people rather than empowerment for justice. A passion for justice flows from encounters with the God of compassion. Contemplation connects the outer world of justice actions with the inner world of the *imago Dei*, God's presence within our hearts.

The journey towards an alternative Christian orthodoxy brings together the three core themes as previously described in Chapter One - the divine, human and cosmos. The convergence of all three elements of the Cosmic Christian Story leads one to an ascent to a higher level of unitive consciousness. A unitive consciousness rejects a mechanistic view of us in the universe and affirms the relationality and interconnectedness of all things within the divine energy of love.

Where and how do you find 'sabbath spaces'?

Joy of the Gospel

Each day, the media highlights a menu of the world's disasters of storms, earthquakes, war, famine, violence and political duplicity. Rarely do good news stories lighten our day. Laughter is exiled from the serious business of living. It would be all too easy to believe that the world is a gloomy place, replete with a succession of disasters. Anxiety is generated by threats of financial meltdowns, a terror alert and health warnings about the next plague.

The Fall/Redemption Story began with God having to restore a failed plan for humanity through the redemptive death of Jesus as the Christ. Sin and failure figure prominently in this story. Humans begin life marked by sin.

The gospel is really Good News. Pope Francis in his encyclical *Evangelii Gaudium* (The Joy of the Gospel) writes, 'The joy of the Gospel is such that it cannot be taken away from us by anyone or anything (cf. Jn. 16:22). The evils of this world – and those of the Church – must not be excuses for diminishing our commitment and our fervour' (84). Although it is helpful to avoid floating in a pollyanna fantasy by looking at the world with rose coloured glasses, we also are aware of the sheer goodness of millions of people doing kind things every day. We are energised by joy. Our spirits are uplifted by people of inspiration and hope. Even within the daily immersions in life struggles, sickness, death and self-doubt, there are blessings everywhere like flowers to be picked on the pathways of each day. There are still spaces for laughter in the stress of each day.

Do we notice and rejoice at the beauty of the flowering of creation? Are we still surprised by the unexpected? Flushed by an act of love? Delight in meeting friends? Do we celebrate community agencies that work for welfare and marvel at the genius of technology? Is a sense of thanksgiving a daily prayer? Above all, do we experience an awareness of the love and intimacy of a God who cares for us: *Can a woman forget her nursing child, or show no compassion for the child of her womb? Even these may forget, yet I will not forget you. See I have inscribed you on the palms of my hands* (Isaiah 49:15 -16)?

Gaze on the palms of your hands and visualise the divine inscription naming you as a blessed one.

Conclusion

This chapter has reflected on important themes in the essence of daily living the Cosmic Christian Story. Ultimately every religious story hopes to enhance a union with God or a divine Presence, 'the Ground of our being'. No one aspect of the Cosmic Christian Story stands alone but is interwoven with the great cosmic story of the universe. Every belief in the alternative orthodoxy cannot do more than lead Christians to the Divine Mystery in Christ who is within and beyond the expanding universe.

A Cosmic Christian Story creed

When you have completed the reading of the chapter, spend some time with companions in composing a CREEDAL STATEMENT or PROFESSION OF FAITH FOR A COSMIC CHRISTIAN STORY which reflects the core themes of an alternative orthodoxy:

As Christians living within the Cosmic Christian Story

We believe...

CHAPTER SEVEN

Gatherings

Then I saw a new heaven and a new earth; for the first heaven and the first earth had passed away and the sea was no more. And I saw the holy city, the new Jerusalem, coming down from heaven from God, prepared as a bride adorned for her husband. And I heard a loud voice from the throne saying, 'See the home of God is among mortals.
He will dwell with them as their God,
And they will be his peoples,
And God himself will be with them'
(Revelation 21:1-3).

A flourishing humanity on a thriving planet, rich in species in an evolving universe, all together filled with the glory of God: such is the vision that must guide us at this critical time of Earth's distress, to practical and critical effect. Ignoring this view keeps people of faith and their churches locked into irrelevance while a terrible drama of life and death is being played out in the real world. By contrast, living the ecological vocation in the power of the Spirit sets us off on a great adventure of mind and heart, expanding the repertoire of our love.

Johnson, E.A. *Ask the Beasts: Darwin and the God of Love*, 286.

This book has sought to reflect on an alternative orthodoxy and spirituality - a Cosmic Christian Story. The spiritual landscape has been changing dramatically during the last few decades. The question is whether Christianity is prepared to return to its primal vision of Jesus and resituate this vision within a cosmic context or persevere in upholding those doctrines and church structures that belong to previous eras. An intentional stance of retaining certain beliefs shaped by a pre-modern world will eventually relegate the church to the relative obscurity of being a marginal influence on world affairs. At this time in human consciousness, the Christian community is being challenged to develop an alternative orthodoxy that incorporates the heritage of Christian wisdoms with the best of proven science within an evolving universe. The Cosmic Christian Story is a complementary story to the Traditional Christian Story.

Modern science and technology offer a new threshold of consciousness for Christianity to enter and reframe its core narrative. The profound sacred myths inherent in the Christ story stimulate imaginative responses to the new questions of life. Those in church leadership who ignore this enterprise will find themselves more and more talking to emptying echo chambers. The cosmic context of the Christ story is the starting point for God's revelation in Jesus as the Christ. The Incarnation is ongoing, both as the advent of Jesus in history and the cosmic Incarnation of God within and outside an expanding universe. Dialogue, scholarship, discourse, listening to the heartbeats of the world and creation itself will ground the Good News in the everyday lives of people.

This time of an emerging consciousness for Christians will be characterised by such themes as:

- being an active citizen for the wellbeing of the earth community;
- fostering an 'abundance of life' wherever possible, especially to the disadvantaged;
- seeking intimacy with a God of love through Jesus and the Spirit;
- promoting ecumenism among religions;
- working towards an eco-centred global partnership for planetary health;
- having a commitment to communal action for justice and peace;
- devising economic systems that share wealth;
- emphasising orthopraxis rather than orthodoxy in living the Christian faith;
- doing theology that is forged from life experiences;
- exploring a global spirituality that includes spiritual wisdoms from many traditions, especially the treasures of Christian spirituality;
- integrating the human story within the scientific story of the universe;
- providing avenues for open conversations and discernment about Church teachings and governance;
- enhancing quality adult life and faith development;
- implementing the full inclusion of women in all levels of church life and wider community;
- modifying hierarchical pyramid structures of the church by empowering the *sensus fidelium* to effectively participate in the leadership of the church;

- sharing the Good News through positive evangelisation;
- celebrating time-honoured worship, devotions and spiritual practices;
- forming welcoming and supportive communities;

And

Celebrating the Joy of the Gospel Through Living as Resurrection People.

For Christians, deification or bringing 'made in the image and likeness of God' to fruition is a positive impulse for encountering God through Christ and the Spirit. In the everyday life of families, work, health, sickness, births and deaths, what does the Cosmic Christian Story mean for living creatively as citizens of the earth community?

The book opened with the question posed by Jesus to his disciples, *Who do you say I am?* After reading the book and reflecting on the question, what now is your response to the question:

Who do you say I am?

The prayer attributed to Paul in Ephesians is a fitting conclusion to the quest for a realisation of being 'made in the image and likeness of God':

For this reason I bow my knees before the Father from whom every family in heaven and on earth takes its name. I pray that, according to the richness of his glory, he may grant that you may be strengthened in your inner being with power through his Spirit, and that Christ may dwell in your hearts through faith, as you are being rooted and grounded in love. I pray that you may have the power to comprehend, and with all the saints, what is the breadth and length and height and depth, and to know the love of Christ that surpasses knowledge, so that you may be filled with all the fullness of God (3:14 -19).

Resources

The resources listed below are only a selection of those used in research for this book:

Armstrong, K. A History of God: *From Abraham to the Present: the 4000-year Quest for God.* London. Vintage Books, 1999.

Armstrong, K. *The Battle for God: a History of Fundamentalism.* New York. The Random House Publishing Group, 2000.

Boeve, L. *Religion after Detraditionalisation: Christian Faith in a Post-Secular Age.* Irish Theological Quarterly 70 (2005), 99-122.

Boeve, L. *Religious Education in a Post-Secular and Post-Christian Context.* Journal of Beliefs and Values: Studies in Religion and Education, 33:2, 143-156. Published online 12th September 2012.

Borg, M.J. *The Heart of Christianity: Rediscovering a Life of Faith.* New York, NY. HarperCollins Publishers, 2003.

Cannato, J. *Field of Compassion: How the New Cosmology is Transforming Spiritual Life.* Notre Dame, Indiana. Sorin Books, 2010.

Carter, Phipps. *Evolutionaries: Unlocking the Spiritual Cultural Potential of Science's Greatest Idea.* New York. Harper Perennial, 2012.

Christensen. M.J. & Wittung, J. A. (eds) *Partakers of the Divine Nature: The History and Development of Deification in the Christian Traditions.* Grand Rapids, Michigan. Baker Academic, 2007.

Church, D. *The Genie in your Genes.* Santa Rosa. Elite Books, 2007.

Cox, B & Cohen, A. *Forces of Nature.* Based on BBC program. BBC, UK, 2016.

Delio, Ilia OSF. *Christ in Evolution.* Maryknoll, New York 10545. Orbis Books, 2008.

Delio, Ilia OSF. *The Emergent Christ: Exploring the Meaning of Catholic in an Evolutionary Universe.* Maryknoll, New York 10545. Orbis Books, 2011.

Delio, Ilia OSF. *Making All Things New: Catholicity, Cosmology, Consciousness.* Maryknoll, New York 10545. Orbis Books, 2015.

Edwards, D. *How God Acts: Creation, Redemption and Special Divine Action.* Hindmarsh SA. ATF Press, 2010.

Edwards, D. *Partaking of God. Trinity, Evolution and Ecology.* Collegeville, Minnesota. Liturgical Press, 2014.

Fox, M. Original Blessing: *A Primer in Creation Spirituality*. Santa Fe, New Mexico. Bear and Company, 1983.

Harari, Y. N. *Sapiens: A Brief History of Humankind*. London. Vintage Books, 2011.

Hunt R.A.E. & Jenks G.C. (eds). *Wisdom and Imagination: Religious Progressives and the Search for Meaning*. Northcote, Vic. Morning Star Publishing, 2014.

Johnson, E. *Women, Earth and Creator Spirit*. Mahwah, New Jersey. Paulist Press, 1993.

Johnson, E.A. *Quest for the Living God: Mapping Frontiers in the Theology of God*. London. Continuum International Publishing Group, 2007.

Johnson, E. A. *Ask the Beasts: Darwin and the God of Love*. London. Bloomsbury Publishing Plc, 2014.

Kelly SJ, T. *Stars, Life and Intelligence: Being a Darwinian and a Believer*. Hindmarsh, SA. ATF Press, 2009.

Kung, H. *The Beginning of All Things: Science and Religion*. Cambridge. Wm. B. Eerdmans Publishing Co, 2007.

Martin, S. *Cosmic Conversations. Dialogues on the Nature of the Universe and the Search for Reality*. Franklin Lakes NJ. New Page Books, 2010.

Merton, T. *New Seeds of Contemplation*. Toronto, Canada. New Directions Paperbook, 1972.

Morwood, M. *It's Time: Challenges to the Doctrine of the Faith*. Charleston, SC. Kelmor Publications, 2013.

Newberg, A. *The Spiritual Brain: Science and the Religious Experience*. Chantilly, VA USA. The Great Courses, 2014.

Newell, J.P. *The New Harmony: The Spirit, The Earth and the Human Soul*. San Francisco. Jossey-Bass. A Wiley Imprint, 2011.

Nowotny-Keane, E. *Amazing Encounters: Direct Communication from the Afterlife*. Kew East, Vic. David Lovell Publishing, 2009.

O'Murchu, D. *Quantum Theology*. New York. The Crossroad Publishing Company, 1997.

O'Murchu, D. *God in the Midst of Change: Wisdom for Confusing Times*. Maryknoll, New York 10545. Orbis Books, 2012.

Panikkar, R. *The Intrareligious Dialogue*. New York, NY. Paulist Press, 1978.

Roughgarden, J. *Evolution and Christian Faith: Reflections of an Evolutionary Biologist*. Hardcover ed. Washington DC. Island Press, 2006.

Schillebeeckx, E. *Ministry: A Case for Change.* London. SCM Press Ltd, 1982.

Smith, A.B. *A New framework for Christian Belief.* London. A CANA Publication, 2001.

Smith, A.B. *God, Energy and the Field.* Winchester, UK. O Books, 2008.

Spong, J.S. *Why Christianity must Change of Die: A Bishop speaks to Believers in Exile.* New York, NY. Harper-Collins, 1999.

Spong, J. S. *Jesus for the Non Religious: Recovering the Divine at the Heart of the Human.* Pymble, NSW Australia. HarperCollins Publishers, 2007.

Tacey, D. *Beyond Literal Belief: Religion as a Metaphor.* Mulgrave, Vic. Australia. Garratt Publishing, 2015.

Tarnas, R. *The Passion of the Western Mind: Understanding the Ideas that have shaped our World View.* New York. Ballantine Books, 1991.

Taylor, C. *A Secular Age.* Harvard. Mass. Harvard University Press, 2007.

Tippett, K. *Becoming Wise: An Inquiry into the Mystery and the Art of Living.* New York. Random House, 2016.

Toews, J. E. *The Story of Original Sin.* Eugene, Or. Pickwick Publications, 2013.

Treston, K. *Emergence for Life, Not Fall from Grace: Making Sense of the Jesus Story in the Light of Evolution.* Northcote, Vic. Morning Star Publishing, 2013.

Turok, N. *The Universe Within: From Quantum to Cosmos.* Sydney, Allen and Unwin, 2013.

Vaugham-Lee, L. *Spiritual Ecology: The Cry of the Earth*: Essays by: Thich Nhat Hanh, Joanna Macey, Wendell Berry, Sandra Ingerman, Richard Rohr, Bill Plotkin, Mary Evelyn Tucker, Brain Swimme, Oren Lyons, Vandana Shiva & Others. The Golden Sufi Centre, California, 2013.

Veli-Matti Karkkainen. *One in God: Salvation as Deification and Justification.* Collegeville, Minnesota. Liturgical Press, 2004.

Wessels, C. *Jesus in the New Universe Story.* Maryknoll, New York. Orbis Books, 2003.

Wilber, K. Integral Spirituality: *A Starting Role for Religion in the Modern and Post Modern World.* Boston and London. Integral Books, 2007

Zagano, P. *Women in Ministry: Emerging Questions about the Diaconate.* New York. Paulist, 2012.

Reflections

The world is in truth a holy place.
Teilhard de Chardin.

God does not love you because you are good. God loves you because God is good.
Richard Rohr

There is nothing better or more necessary than love.
St John of the Cross

What a person takes in by contemplation, that person pours out in love.
Meister Eckhart

When you walk with naked feet, how can you forget the earth?
Carl Jung.

All shall be well and all shall be well and all manner of things shall be well.
Julian of Norwich.

Whoever is not enlightened by the splendour of created things is blind; whoever is not aroused by the sound of their voice is deaf; whoever does not praise God for all these creatures is mute; whoever, after so much evidence, does not recognise the maker of all things, is an idiot .
St Bonaventure

We shall not cease from exploration
And the end of all our exploring
Will be to arrive where we started
And know the place for the first time.
T.S. Elliot

The mountains, I became part of it
The herbs, the fir tree, I became part of it
The morning mists, the clouds, the gathering waters,
I became part of it
The wilderness, the dew drops, the pollen
I became part of it.
Navajo Chant

To live, you must choose; to love you must encounter; to grow you must suffer.
Victor Frankl, Holocaust survivor.

Problems cannot be solved by the same level of thinking that created them.
Albert Einstein

Everything that is in the heavens, in the earth, and under the earth is penetrated with connectedness, penetrated with relatedness.
Hildegard of Bingen

There are only two ways to live your life. One is that nothing is a miracle. The other is that everything is a miracle.
Albert Einstein

Every day, priests minutely examine the Law and endlessly chant complicated sutras.
Before doing that, though, they should learn
How to read the love letters sent by the wind
And rain, the snow and the moon.
Ikkyu

Turning and turning in the widening gyre
The falcon cannot hear the falconer;
Things fall apart; the centre cannot hold;
Mere anarchy is loosed upon the world...
Surely some revelation is at hand.
William Butler Yeats *The Second Coming*

God is an intelligible space whose centre is everywhere and whose circumference is nowhere... (God) is within all things, but not enclosed, outside all things, but not excluded, above all things but not aloof, below all things but not debased.
St Bonaventure

For it was you who formed my inward parts;
You knit me together in my mother's womb.
I praise you, for I am fearfully and wonderfully made.
Wonderful are your works;
That I know very well.
Psalm 139 13 - 14